GETTING YOUR MSW

Also Available from Lyceum Books, Inc.

GETTING YOUR MSW:
HOW TO SURVIVE AND THRIVE IN A SOCIAL WORK PROGRAM

Karen M. Sowers
University of Tennessee

Bruce A. Thyer
Florida State University

LYCEUM
BOOKS, INC.

Chicago, Illinois

© Lyceum Books, Inc., 2006

Published by

Lyceum Books, Inc.
5758 S. Blackstone Ave.
Chicago, Illinois 60637
773+643-1903 (Fax)
773+643-1902 (Phone)
lyceum@lyceumbooks.com
http://www.lyceumbooks.com

10 9 8 7 6 5 4 3 2 1

ISBN 0-925065-70-6

Library of Congress Cataloging-in-Publication Data

Sowers, Karen M. (Karen Marlaine)
    Getting your MSW : how to survive and thrive in a social work
program / by Karen Sowers and Bruce Thyer.
        p. cm.
    Includes bibliographical references and indexes.
    ISBN 0-925065-70-6
    1. Social work education—United States. 2. Social service—Vocational
guidance—United States. I. Title: How to survive and thrive in a social
work program. II. Thyer, Bruce A. III. Title.
HV11.7.S68   2005
361.3'071'173—dc22

                                                              2005010263

CONTENTS

ABOUT THE AUTHORS

Karen M. Sowers, (MSW, Florida State University; PhD, Florida State University) is professor in and dean of the College of Social Work at the University of Tennessee. She served as director of the School of Social Work at Florida International University from June 1994 to August 1997 and as undergraduate program director of the School of Social Work at Florida International University from 1986 to 1994. Professor Sowers is nationally known for her research and scholarship in the areas of juvenile justice, child welfare, cultural diversity, international social work practice, and social work education. Her current research and community interests include evidence-based practice, best practices in mental health, competency based social work education, international social work practice, and juvenile justice. She has authored and coauthored numerous books and book chapters and has refereed journal articles. She is a founding member of the Journal *Research on Social Work Practice* and is the founding coeditor of *Best Practices in Mental Health: An International Journal*. She also serves on the editorial boards of the *Journal of Evidence-Based Social Work: Advances in Practice, Programs, Research and Policy* and the *Journal of Stress, Trauma and Crisis: An International Journal*.

Bruce A. Thyer, (MSW, University of Georgia; PhD, University of Michigan) is professor of social work and former dean of the School of Social Work at Florida State University. Professor Thyer earned a PhD in Social Work and Psychology, and he was an LCSW. He has served on the faculties of the University of Michigan, the University of Georgia, and Florida State University. Professor Thyer is married to fellow social worker Laura Myers. Included in their coauthorships are their four children, John, age 11, William, 9, Joseph, 8, and Cynthia, 5.

PREFACE

Many years ago, when we (the authors, Karen Sowers and Bruce Thyer) were beginning our own MSW programs, we fervently wished for some sort of guidebook that would help explain things for beginning graduate students like ourselves. We wanted a book that would help orient us to the field of social work in general, but more importantly one that would help us to understand the organization of MSW education, who the major players were at the national level, and something about the structure of our own MSW program. We also looked in vain for some resources to help us get settled into life as graduate students, a distinctly different existence than that of being an undergraduate, or a paid, full-time employee.

Now, several decades later, we are fairly well settled as members of the very establishment into which we took such tentative and uncertain steps. Karen is professor of social work and dean of the College of Social Work at the University of Tennessee, and Bruce is professor of social work and former dean of the College of Social Work at Florida State University. Both institutions are major research and teaching universities with thriving MSW programs. Both of us have crawled up through the social work academic evolutionary scale—new MSW student, agency-based practitioner, PhD student, then assistant, then associate (with tenure!), and now full professor.

Karen was previously the director of the social work program at Florida International University, and Bruce administered the MSW Admissions Office at the University of Georgia and served as director of the UGA social work PhD program. Between the two of us we have served on most significant committees within a typical school of social work (curriculum, admissions, grade appeals, practicum, student affairs, etc.) and larger university context (promotion and tenure, appeals, etc.). Also, between the two of us we have been social work faculty at seven different universities or colleges—Winthrop College in South Carolina, Florida International University in North Miami, University of Tennessee, University of Michigan, Florida State University, University of Georgia, and the University of Huddersfield in the United Kingdom. We have also served in a variety of positions in social work's major professional associations—the National Association of Social Workers, the Council on Social Work Education, the Group for the Advancement of Doctoral Education in Social Work, the American Association of State Social Work Boards, and the Society for Social Work and Research, among other groups. These diverse experiences have given us a solid and comprehensive perspective of the situations and challenges facing the prospective and current MSW student.

Although we admit to being middle-aged, we are not so old as to have forgotten the trials and tribulations, anxieties and ecstasies of graduate student life. Indeed, we constantly relive these experiences vicariously in our everyday role as teachers watching the lives of our MSW students unfold. So when the opportunity came for us to author this guide to surviving one's MSW program, we eagerly accepted the challenge, thinking of how incredibly useful such a book would be for today's graduate student.

There are a number of other types of graduate school survival guides. For example, we strongly recommend *The Women's Guide to Surviving Graduate School* (Rittner & Trudeau, 1997), *The African American Student's Guide to Surviving Graduate School* (Isaac, 1998), *Completing Graduate School Long Distance* (Hammon & Albiston, 1998), and *Surviving Graduate School Part Time* (Pittman, 1997), as these all contain useful generic information and also content about their particular title. However, there was no such volume that specifically dealt with the field of social work, hence the present book.

This book's organization mirrors your real-life timeline as an MSW student—beginning with advice on how to select the MSW program that is right for you; how to apply; how to prepare for enrollment; how to best adjust to living in a new school, university, and community; getting oriented to the MSW curriculum; taking advantage of existing support services provided by your school of social work and university; getting involved in relevant professional organizations; and, as you near the end of your program of study, finding a job and getting licensed.

Although some people look at the time you spend in graduate school as a gap or time-out from full involvement in the adventure of life, we are of the strong opinion that the twelve to twenty-four months you spend as an MSW student are part and parcel of living, in its fullest sense. You will work, play, develop new relationships (and perhaps have some established ones fall apart), have children, be involved with your families, and do a great deal of studying. For some, in years to come you will look fondly back upon this time as one of the most exciting, vibrant, and challenging periods of your life. It certainly was for us. Although for other readers (hopefully only a few), it may turn out to be an unmitigated series of one horror after another. We hope not, and by preparing this volume for your use we hope that you will be able to avoid some avoidable blunders and cushion the blows of the inevitable ones.

We have deliberately chosen to avoid a lofty, academic tone in our writing. We wanted to make reading this volume as user-friendly as possible, using the honest, open language and forthrightness we would use if we were chatting at a downtown coffeehouse with a niece or nephew who was considering earning the MSW or who had already enrolled in such a program. Although the written book format does not lend itself very readily to a dialog between you and us, we do encourage you to write or E-mail us with comments and suggestions intended to improve a future edition. We wrote this book for you, and we respectfully dedicate this volume to the past, present, and future generations of MSW students from whom we have learned so much.

Karen M. Sowers
Bruce A. Thyer

References

Hammon, D. L., & Albiston, S. K. (1998). *Completing graduate school long distance.* Thousand Oaks, CA: Sage.

Isaac, A. (1998). *The African American student's guide to surviving graduate school.* Thousand Oaks, CA: Sage.

Pittman, V. (1997). *Surviving graduate school part time.* Thousand Oaks, CA: Sage.

Rittner, B., & Trudeau, P. (1997). *The women's guide to surviving graduate school.* Thousand Oaks, CA: Sage.

Chapter 1

SELECTING THE
RIGHT MSW PROGRAM

We begin our book assuming that you have already decided that a career as a professional social worker with a graduate degree is the right one for you. Perhaps you have already earned a Bachelor of Social Work (BSW) and have decided to pursue the master's degree. Or maybe you are a liberal arts graduate and want to work in the human services after earning the Master of Social Work (MSW). You could be in school now, completing a bachelor's degree, or perhaps you are returning to school after an absence of some years. Regardless of such factors, you will be warmly welcomed into graduate school and into the community of practitioners, researchers, and scholars who collectively comprise the social work profession.

If you do not know much about social work, you would be well advised to read some further information about this fascinating and challenging field before enrolling in graduate school. The major professional group of social workers is the National Association of Social Workers (NASW), and they produce a very informative brochure called *Careers in Social Work* (NASW, 1997), which you should read in order to get a brief overview of the kinds of jobs social workers do. You can contact the NASW by mail using the following contact information: National Association of Social Workers, 750 First Street, NE, Suite 700, Washington, DC 20002-4241; 800-638-8799 toll free. The Web page, www.naswdc.org, is also a good way to contact the NASW.

Another very good resource is a book, also called *Careers in Social Work* (Ginsberg, 1998), which is packed with information about what social work *is,* the types of jobs open to MSW graduates, typical salaries, and other useful information that can help you learn more about the field. Your local university library or career planning and placement office may have a copy, or you can order it from any bookstore or over the Web.

You can also call the state chapter of the National Association of Social Workers and ask them to put you in touch with local practicing social workers to discuss their work in the field.

These resources can help you to gain a more accurate understanding of the diversity associated with the social work profession. Although social workers continue to play important roles in fields traditionally associated with the discipline—areas such as welfare, child protection, foster care and adoption, and public health—in recent decades clinical social workers have come to dominate the mental health field. For example, in 1998 a national survey conducted by a federal agency found that there were at least 192,814 clinically trained social workers, more than the number of psychiatric nurses (17,318), clinical psychologists (73,018), and psychiatrists (33,486) combined (see O'Neill, 1999). These MSW graduates are often employed in community mental health centers, elementary and secondary schools, hospitals, the correctional system, and in private practice.

This diversity of employment opportunities is a particularly attractive aspect of holding an MSW degree. Here are two extreme examples. Gerald Hogarty, MSW, (he does not hold a doctorate degree) is Professor of Psychiatry at the University of Pittsburgh School of Medicine. Professor Hogarty has, for several decades, designed, conducted, and published randomized controlled clinical trials of psychoeducational and psychopharmacological interventions intended to help individuals with chronic mental illness. He has received numerous large research grants from the federal government and is widely recognized as one of the world's foremost clinical researchers in the field of schizophrenia. At the opposite end of the spectrum of social work positions, we find Senator Barbara Mikulski, MSW, who has been a United States senator for many years, representing the state of Maryland. Here is what she has said about her career as a national leader in the field of federal welfare and social policy:

> I am the first social worker in the U.S. Senate. Now I have a caseload of 4 million Marylanders. And although I am practicing in a different forum, those skills and values I learned as a community organizer in the streets of Baltimore are what make me an effective leader in the corridors of Congress. (NASW, 1993, p. 31)

2

As you can see, there are many different opportunities for people with an MSW degree but not a PhD.

IS SOCIAL WORK RIGHT FOR ME?

There are many different descriptions of social work. It is a profession with great breadth and varied specialties and can be characterized as a comprehensive helping profession. Despite the breadth and versatility of the profession, social workers do share certain commonalities. As a profession, we are concerned with helping people to learn how to interact more effectively with the world around them and simultaneously change that world to make it more supportive of human welfare. At its core, social work attends to the quality of people's social functioning (Morales & Sheafor, 2001). There are five themes which characterize social work. They are: 1) a commitment to social betterment, 2) a goal to enhance social functioning, 3) an action orientation, 4) an appreciation for human diversity, and 5) a versatile practice perspective. An examination of these themes can help you ascertain if you are well suited to be a social worker. Do your qualities, abilities, and talents fit well with these themes? Do you believe in the importance of improving the quality of social interaction for all people and helping people enhance their social functioning? Are you an action-oriented person who would enjoy a "hands-on" profession, working with people, groups, families, communities, agencies, and organizations? Do you have an appreciation for diversity in all its forms, including diversity of persons, knowledge and skills, cultures, and applications? Can you value the unique perspectives of persons of different gender, sexual orientation, or age groups? Are you open to learning a wide variety of approaches to work effectively with diverse populations?

What Are the Demographics of the Profession?

The profession of social work comprises people from diverse backgrounds. People of every gender, sexual orientation, age, culture, race, and physical ability constitute our profession. The number of women tends to outweigh the number of men in the profession today, and, as a result, many schools of social work strategically recruit men. Because social work places a high value on diversity, you will find that the profession welcomes and embraces persons from a variety of backgrounds. This includes racial and ethnic minorities, gays, lesbians, bisexual and transgendered persons, as well as persons with disabilities.

What Is the Job Market Like in Social Work?

More than one hundred years old in the United States, the profession of social work has a strong foundation. However, social programs and the actual job market differ throughout the country. As with every profession, the availability of jobs fluctuates with economic conditions in geographical areas. However, there is a great availability of interesting social work jobs across the nation and across the globe.

But enough of the sales pitch on becoming a social worker, and on to the nuts and bolts of actually deciding where to go to graduate school. Roughly speaking, there are four major factors that should figure into your decision-making process: 1) the quality of the school of social work itself, 2) whether the MSW program is CSWE-accredited, 3) the quality of the larger university which hosts the school of social work, and 4) the quality of the larger community wherein the university itself is placed. Let's look at each of these individually.

WHAT YOU SHOULD KNOW ABOUT SOCIAL WORK PROGRAMS AND WHERE TO START

A good place to begin is to write the school of social work (SSW) where you are contemplating enrolling and ask them for a copy of their catalog and MSW application forms. They should send these things to you for free. Read these materials carefully and see if there is a good fit between your interests and what the school offers. Another option is to check out the school of social work's (some programs are called Departments of Social Work, but this distinction is of little importance in deciding where to go to graduate school) Web site. Often, you can view catalogs or download application forms directly from the Web site.

Is the MSW Program CSWE-Accredited?

In our opinion, the primary feature to look for when considering a graduate SSW is to see if it is fully accredited by an organization called the Council on Social Work Education (CSWE). To place this issue in context, you need to realize that in order to eventually be licensed as a social worker, you need to have earned an MSW from a graduate SSW accredited by the CSWE. The CSWE is the *only* agency authorized by the Council for Higher Education Accreditation (CHEA), the umbrella agency that is responsible for determining which organizations shall serve to accredit various professional training programs. The CHEA is the successor organization to an older group called the Commission on Recognition of Postsecondary Accreditation (CORPA), and CHEA itself receives its mandate from the United States Department of Education.

Do not let all these acronyms and agencies confuse you. The issue is really quite simple, and most SSW bulletins clearly state something to the effect of, "The school of social work is fully accredited by the Council on Social Work Education." If this is not readily apparent in the printed materials, simply call the program and ask them. If the answer is no, your choice is simple. *Do not* enroll in that program.

A few newer programs may have received "candidacy" accreditation by the CSWE. This accreditation means that they have been given the go ahead by the CSWE to begin offering a program of study leading to the MSW. In such cases, full accreditation is almost always earned after one or two classes of MSW students graduate, with recognition of full accreditation retroactively extending to these early graduates. Thus, a rating of candidacy accreditation should not deter you from giving serious consideration to attending a developing program. Another category is labeled "provisional" accreditation, a rating given to graduate programs in social work that had some significant deficiencies emerge during their last accreditation review conducted by the CSWE (these occur about every seven years). Usually, schools of social work make strenuous efforts to remedy any problems that led to them being only provisionally accredited, and full accreditation is usually forthcoming after a year or so of provisional status. MSW students graduating during this provisional period are treated by state licensure bodies and employers as having earned a fully-accredited degree, provided that full accreditation is subsequently awarded to the SSW by the CSWE following a limited period of provisional accreditation. However rarely, it does happen that an MSW program that initially receives a provisional accreditation eventually loses its accreditation by the CSWE, and the graduates of such a SSW are placed in a seriously disadvantaged position, to put it delicately. You may have some compelling personal, logistical, or financial reasons for enrolling in a provisionally accredited MSW program, but if you choose to do so, go into the situation knowing that there is a small possibility that accreditation may eventually be completely lost. Generally, it would be wise to avoid enrolling in such a SSW. A complete list of accredited programs as well as those in candidacy can be found at www.cswe.org. However, if you are unsure about the accreditation status of a program, it is best to contact the school directly.

Here is a worst case scenario: you enroll in a school of social work that is simply unaccredited by the Council on Social Work Education (there are very few floating around). You work very hard for a couple years, graduate with your MSW, but find, to your dismay, that you cannot obtain employment in the state or federal sector, or even among most of the private employers, due to the lack of CSWE accreditation of your degree. Is this horrible prospect possible? Yes, unfortunately. Read on:

> The president of a Louisiana correspondence college that granted thousands of unaccredited degrees, including degrees in social work, pleaded guilty to fraud in November. Thomas J. Kirk is to be sentenced this month for conspiring to commit mail and credit card fraud and evade taxes in connection with the operation of the World Christian Church and LaSalle University in Mandeville, LA. . . . LaSalle's social work program was not accredited by the Council on Social Work Education, making a degree earned from that school virtually worthless for gaining a state social work license. Kirk admitted as part of his guilty plea that he conspired to commit fraud by misleading prospective students and telling them that the school was accredited by a fictitious organization named the Council on Postsecondary Christian Education. (NASW, 1997, p. 9)

The best protection is gained by attending only a fully CSWE-accredited MSW program.

The CSWE does not rank schools of social work in terms of their quality. Accreditation by CSWE simply means that the school complies with certain basic standards expected of professional training programs in social work. The existing ranking studies, such as those published periodically by the *U.S. News and World Report*, use ranking methodologies that are of dubious scientific credibility and should not be strongly relied on as indicators of genuine excellence.

In reading SSW bulletins, you may find that the actual name of the degree varies somewhat. Most schools offer the Master of Social Work (MSW), but a few award the Master of Science in Social Work (MSSW, offered by the University of Tennessee), the Master of Science in Social Administration (MSSA, offered by Case Western Reserve University), or simply the AM (Artium Magister's, which is Latin for Master of Arts, offered by the University of Chicago) in social work. Do not let this worry you. As long as the degree is fully accredited by the CSWE, they are considered to be equivalent by social work professional associations and regulatory bodies. For convenience, we shall refer to all schools granting such CSWE-accredited degrees as MSW programs.

How Can I Learn about Programs?

One of your first hurdles will be learning about the simple existence of accredited graduate programs. You have several options. The aforementioned book *Careers in Social Work* (Ginsberg, 1998) lists each accredited program but does not provide mailing addresses. The Council on Social Work Education issues a brochure every few years that lists the names, addresses, and phone numbers of all accredited and provisionally accredited MSW programs. To obtain a copy of this brochure, you can write to them at: Council on Social Work Education, 1600 Duke Street, Suite 300, Alexandria, VA 22314-3421; call 703-683-8080, or fax 703-683-8099.

An easier way to get information is to check out the CSWE Web page, www.cswe.org. We strongly encourage you to review this site, as it is packed with useful information. The site contains a directory with the names, addresses, and phone numbers of all MSW programs, organized by state. So, for instance, if you wished to attend an MSW program located in the southeastern portion of the United States, then you would click on, say, Georgia, and find out how to contact the programs offered in that state; then check out the offerings in Tennessee, South Carolina, Florida, etc.

Apart from the Web page resources, the CSWE publishes the *Directory of Colleges and Universities with Accredited Social Work Degree Programs.* This brochure is updated periodically, and it costs about $13 to order the hardcopy document from the CSWE (you can order it over the Internet if you wish, or call the organization directly).

Although the CSWE does not qualitatively rank the various schools of social work, it also publishes a monograph titled *Summary Information on Master of Social Work Programs.* This monograph costs about $15 and provides information about each school's tuition and other charges, how long it takes to complete the MSW, the concentrations or specializations offered, the types of field practica (i.e., internships) offered to students, and whether or not the school has an abbreviated program of study for graduates with an accredited BSW degree (more on this a bit later). This monograph can be ordered directly from the CSWE by mail, phone, or the Web page. Be aware, however, that the information contained in this resource can rapidly grow out of date as tuition costs escalate, curricula are modified, and new concentrations are offered and old ones discontinued. So be sure to get a current SSW bulletin from any program to which you are seriously considering applying.

The Peterson's Publishing Company publishes annual reference books describing graduate programs in various disciplines; the one most relevant to your interests would be *Peterson's Graduate Programs in Business, Education, Health, Information Studies, & Social Work* (Peterson's, 1997). Find the most recent edition (preferably no more than a year or two old) to learn lots of information about MSW programs. Just about all accredited programs will be mentioned, and quite a few will have lengthier listings containing much detail. The Web page www.petersons.com should have directions for ordering the latest edition if your local library does not have one. Other Internet-based resources are the Web pages developed by the various schools of social work. With a little exploring on the Web, you can find them.

What Is the Program's Rating?

Some external organizations or authors have developed various rankings of schools of social work, such as the well-known rankings published annually in the magazine *U.S. News and World Report.* In general, these ratings are of unknown value. In most cases these rankings represent the cumulative ratings provided by the deans and directors of schools of social work from all over the country. However, that's like asking automobile dealers to rate the quality of all the various cars and trucks sold in America. Perhaps a better approach would be to ask the drivers of automobiles, or, for our purposes, the students and graduates of MSW programs, but to our knowledge no one has undertaken this type of effort.

Other ratings of schools of social work have been taken in terms of the scholarly productivity of the faculty affiliated with each school (e.g., Ligon, Thyer, & Dixon, 1995). Unfortunately, you cannot really rely on how frequently a faculty person publishes in professional journals as a sound indicator of the quality of training in social work practice that you will be exposed to, which, after all, should be your primary consideration. A prolific writer may not be a great teacher, or, if she is a great instructor, she may teach relatively few classes (because she is so busy writing).

Some MSW programs distribute news releases or other announcements indicating that they were highly ranked in a given study. Do not be too impressed by these announcements, as such ratings will likely have little bearing on the quality of your training.

Is Advanced Standing Offered?

Individuals with a BSW degree may qualify for entry into an abbreviated program of study leading to the MSW degree. The requirements for acceptance into an "advanced standing" program vary from school to school, but if this option is offered it generally involves having earned a BSW from a CSWE-accredited program within the last five years, having an overall undergraduate GPA of no less than 2.5 on a 4-point scale, and having earned an overall GPA of no less than 3.0 for all social work classes.

Advanced standing usually means you can skip the first and second semesters of the traditional two-year program of study leading to the MSW and enroll the summer before the second year of the program of study begins. Thus, instead of attending four full semesters, the usual configuration required to earn the MSW, advanced standing students can earn the degree by attending a summer session followed by the usual two full semesters (the second year of the program of study). But keep in mind that schools of social work do vary on how they offer advanced standing. Some only require attending during the fall and winter semesters and do not require enrolling for a summer term. Advanced standing can be a great arrangement; so if you qualify for it, consider its advantages.

Keep in mind, though, that not all schools of social work offer the advanced standing option and that the qualifications for it can greatly vary among those that do. You may wonder whether or not MSW graduates who earned their degree via an advanced standing program are as well prepared to enter practice as those who completed the traditional full two-year program of study. This question has concerned academics and practitioners since advanced standing began to be offered. The available evidence permits the tentative conclusion that advanced standing graduates are as well prepared as those completing lengthier programs (see Carrillo & Thyer, 1994; Thyer, Vonk, & Tandy, 1996), but a definitive answer to this issue is not yet available. The advantages in terms of saving time and money certainly make the advanced standing option very attractive to those who qualify for it; thus, whether or not a particular program offers this option may figure into your decision about where to go. Students with a liberal arts or other non-BSW undergraduate degree are not permitted to enroll in advanced standing programs. But do keep in mind that the majority of students enrolling in MSW programs do not have a BSW degree—most have a degree with a substantial liberal arts component, with majors like psychology, sociology, and education being particularly common.

Can I Complete the Program on a Part-time Basis?

You may wish to choose between completing your MSW on a full-time basis versus attending a part-time program. Many programs offer you the opportunity to earn the MSW on a part-time basis. Again, this information will be available in each school's program bulletin. By attending on a part-time basis you may be able to keep your regular employment because many part-time programs offer coursework during the evenings and/or weekends and are tailored to the needs of a busy professional like you. The book *Surviving Graduate School Part*

Time (Pittman, 1997) would be a useful reference for MSW applicants considering going to graduate school on a part-time basis. By going full-time you will graduate sooner rather than later, feel more like the traditional graduate student, and have a greater sense of integration with faculty and the university community. However, if you can only arrange to attain an MSW by going on a part-time basis, then by all means proceed with that option, as this would be preferable to not being able to enroll at all. The jury is still out on the relative merits of part-time versus full-time MSW training in terms of education quality (see Gatz, Patten, Thyer, & Parrish, 1990). Our practical advice is to do what is best for you.

Can Portions of the MSW Program Be Taken "At a Distance"?

Another variable may be the availability of selected coursework offered on a distance learning basis. Distance learning instruction may occur through a variety of media, including two-way interactive televised live instruction, videotaped coursework, coursework offered using the Web, and by having faculty travel to teaching sites away from the home campus to teach a class of students in person. The available distance learning course offerings may reduce some of your costs, maybe not tuition, but certainly commuting and the physical wear and tear of travel.

An increasing number of schools offer distance learning coursework, and electing to take such classes may make completing your MSW a much more feasible undertaking. Like the advanced standing issue, the comparability of the quality of training received by distance learning students versus those sitting through class with a live instructor has been a source of moderate controversy within the field of academic social work. Very few quality studies have examined this issue with respect to social work training. Some of those that have looked at the issue have found that generally distance learning students are less satisfied with the quality of instruction received via television, compared to being taught in person (e.g., Thyer, Polk, & Gaudin, 1997; Thyer, Artelt, Markward, & Dozier, 1998). However, satisfaction with instruction does not necessarily translate into poorer quality training, so the jury is still out with this issue.

Recently Florida State University began an online part-time MSW program, open only to individuals with a BSW degree. Students take two online courses per semester using an interactive Internet system called Blackboard, and when coursework is completed, the students undertake a standard live internship in a local social work agency with real clients and on-site supervisors. This novel program is being carefully evaluated, and it may be offered in the near future to nonresidents of Florida.

Many SSWs offer MSW coursework, and even entire MSW programs, at smaller campuses located some distance from the home campus. These too can be a useful way for people to enroll in and complete an MSW program.

Is Specialized Training Available?

In terms of training, you should know that most schools of social work offer a generalist MSW degree and that few offer intense, formally organized specializations in particular fields of practice. (Actually for a variety of reasons the CSWE discourages specialization training during MSW programs.) For example, if you really wish to have a career focusing on helping sexually abused children, it is unlikely that you will find a school of social work that offers a formal program of study in this area. However, many will offer "tracks" focusing on broader fields, such as child welfare, or practice with children and adolescents. Then, through careful selection of elective coursework and choice of term paper topics, you may well be able to center your studies around your long-term field of interest. But this may require some clever and creative maneuvering on your part.

Exceptions to the above do exist, however. Some schools do offer concentrations in clinical social work and mental health, others in policy or community practice, etc. Again, you are well served by a careful review of the program descriptions found in the individual SSW bulletins. Another common option is for a SSW to offer an optional certificate program of some form of advanced study for MSW students to complete. Sometimes these certificates can be completed within the time frame and constraints of the core MSW program, but sometimes they may require an additional semester (or even more) of coursework and/or internship. At the Florida State University School of Social Work,

12

students can complete optional certificate programs in gerontology, marriage and family therapy, and the arts in psychotherapy. So be sure to peruse the SSW bulletins to see if there are any of these types of additional certifications available to you. And of course, inquire very carefully about their practical value. For example, in Georgia individuals holding their licenses as clinical social workers are permitted by law to engage in the practice of marital and family therapy (that is true in most states), rendering the optional certificate in MFT, which requires an additional term of study to complete, a less attractive option.

What Types of Internships Are Available?

Related to the possibility of specialization may be the opportunities provided within each SSW for what has been called field instruction but what is increasingly being labeled practicum or internship training. Bottom line, the CSWE mandates that all MSW programs require that each two-year-program student complete at least nine hundred clock hours of internship, usually provided within the context of a local community or human services agency. One's internship is usually obtained in two different agencies, one during the first year of the MSW program and in a second, different one during the second year of instruction (advanced standing students, of course, complete only the second-year internship). Look at the listing of agencies (usually found within the SSW bulletin) that recently hosted MSW students during their internship experiences. It may be that you have your heart set on interning at a particular agency used as an internship site by your potential SSW. You may opt to enroll in a particular MSW program solely because of this potential internship agency. However, keep in mind that agreements between SSW and local agencies are constantly being renegotiated, and agencies available one year may not be available the next year. Also, some MSW programs assign students to internship agencies, particularly for their field year of placement, and you may not be able to get your first choice. Try to find out from the bulletin about the extent to which your wishes are followed with respect to practicum assignments. We do not recommend that you attend a particular school solely because of the potential of being assigned to a particular internship site.

Your internship experience is a crucial aspect of your training as a social work professional, equally as significant as classroom instruction and in some ways, especially in terms of acquiring clinical skills, even more so.

What about the Faculty?

Similar considerations apply with respect to wanting to study with a particular professor. Let's say that the State University School of Social Work is where Professor Mary Richmond teaches, and that Professor Richmond is a world renowned scholar in a practice area of particular interest to you. Should you apply to State University in the hopes of working directly with Professor Richmond, having her as your academic advisor, taking her classes, receiving one-on-one supervision from her, maybe even becoming her protégé? In a word, no. Professor Richmond may already have a pretty full plate and may not be able to provide you with the individual attention and tutoring you crave. She may be on sabbatical next year, teach only in the doctoral program, or go on to take a position at another SSW. She might even retire before you even begin your program. To avoid this kind of situation, you should write her directly and inquire about the possibility of your having much contact with her as you navigate the MSW program. If she indicates that you can choose her as your advisor, take plenty of courses with her, have her be your faculty liaison when you are in internship, and that she will work with you on a research project or thesis, then by all means apply to the SSW where she teaches. But check out this possibility before applying, moving across the country, and enrolling at State University in order to work with Professor Richmond. This preparation can help you to avoid some disappointments.

The SSW bulletins will usually list all their faculty. Most (if not all) should have earned an MSW degree themselves, and most should have a doctorate in social work or a closely related field. It is not uncommon for the majority of social work faculty to have the MSW and a doctorate in something else (e.g., education, psychology, sociology, public administration, etc.). Unfortunately, too few individuals graduate each year with a doctorate in social work to fill the available SSW faculty openings, which necessitates the hiring of individuals without doctorates in social work. And, of course, there may well be significant advantages to being taught by faculty with such dual credentials, as they can lend a refreshing interdisciplinary perspective to your studies.

If you are particularly concerned with the quality of clinical training you may receive at a given SSW, inquire about the proportion of faculty who maintain their current state license as a clinical social worker. Regrettably, social work education standards do not require that teachers of practice themselves possess a license to practice in the state in which they teach. However, this need not deter you (as a potential consumer) from inquiring about this variable when deciding where to go to graduate school.

Does the Program Offer Information Sessions?

Sometimes a SSW will offer optional information sessions to potential applicants or to those already accepted into the MSW program. Sometimes these sessions can be useful vehicles for you to have many of your questions answered. Related to these are events, generically called Graduate School and Career Days, usually held at the student center or some other convenient location on a university or college campus. These rooms are often filled with convention-style booths staffed by helpful MSW admissions faculty and graduate students who are eager and willing to tell you all about their particular graduate program and why you should apply to their SSW. Sometimes you can hit a dozen or more MSW programs in a single afternoon at the larger of these events, coming away with totebags full of SSW bulletins, admission applications, and financial aid packages. The career planning and placement center at your local college or university can provide you with a schedule of such events. Obviously these career planning and placement events will be more frequent, and larger, in major metropolitan areas like New York City, Boston, Chicago, and Los Angeles, areas with several nearby universities, than in a more rural area.

How Much Does It Cost to Attend?

Tuition and other costs may be significant factors when you choose an MSW program. Schools of social work at private colleges and universities (e.g., Columbia University, University of Chicago, Washington University) and the best public ones (e.g., University of Michigan, University of California at Berkeley, University of Washington) can be very expensive, particularly for out-of-state residents, compared to the second- or third-tier schools of social work. Many of the top schools are in metropolitan areas, which can greatly increase even simple living expenses. A limited income in Manhattan, Kansas, goes a lot further than the same amount of money in Manhattan, New York.

We recommend that you, the poor but honest reader of this book, apply to several of the most competitive schools, along with applying for financial aid. If accepted, see what is provided in the way of financial aid. Then make up your mind about where to enroll. Do not exclude yourself from even applying to, say, the Ivory Tower University School of Social Work, merely because it costs $30,000, because Ivory Tower University may offer you a scholarship for $29,000, meaning that you have to come up with only $1,000 out of pocket. At the same time, apply to the equivalents of State University, where tuition is $4,000 per year but may offer you nothing in the way of scholarship money. Thus, attending Ivory Tower University (in this very fictitious illustration) could cost less than enrolling in State University's program. The above are exaggerations of the general idea of encouraging you to apply to the best school of social work you think you can get into and not be deterred by financial considerations until all the facts (i.e., the financial aid package they offer you) are in. Only then are you in a reasonable position to judge whether or not you can afford the better SSW.

Do not plan to attend a public university in another state for a year and then expect to be successful in applying for residency status for tuition-paying purposes your second year. The administrative and policy hurdles universities place in the path of students seeking in-state residency status are formidable, and usually you will not be successful. Voting in your new state, registering your car there, and paying income taxes all count for little in redetermining your residency status with the graduate school of your university. One of the few things you can do is marry a state resident (a rather drastic measure if done solely for the purposes of reducing one's out-of-state tuition) or buy a home. The graduate school can provide further details of what it would take to be classified as a resident, and you should find out in advance of enrollment what the actual policy is at the out-of-state school you are contemplating attending, as this may have a bearing on your decision to attend.

Does the Program Offer a Joint Degree?

You may be interested in pursuing a dual master's program, or some other combination of master's/professional degree, as a part of your MSW program. There are a limited number of such opportunities available, with the MSW being jointly offered with a Master of Public Health (MPH), Master of Business Administration (MBA), Master of Public Administration (MPA), Juris Doctor (JD), or Master of Divinity (MDiv) at various universities. The usual arrangement is that you apply for admission to both programs concurrently and must be accepted into both. Then, you either complete course requirements at the same time, or consecutively (first one, then the other), with the opportunity to have some coursework count toward both degrees, resulting in an ultimate savings in time and expense. Also, more than a dozen schools of social work offer joint MSW/PhD programs, wherein you are admitted into the doctoral program at the same time you begin your MSW studies. Again, there is usually some savings of coursework, which makes admission to a joint degree program more efficient than completing the MSW and then enrolling in a doctoral program thereafter. Schools that offer this joint MSW/PhD option include the University of Michigan, Michigan State University, and Boston University, among others.

The number of dual degree and joint degree programs changes from year to year, and there is no comprehensive listing of them, so your best bet is simply to review the SSW bulletins of universities you are interested in attending to see if such options are available. Another option is to check out the Web page on social work doctoral programs maintained by the Group for the Advancement of Doctoral Education at web.uconn.edu/gade. Each social work doctoral program has its own couple of pages, and whether or not they offer a joint MSW/PhD program is clearly indicated.

CHARACTERISTICS OF THE UNIVERSITY

Big universities have many significant advantages over small colleges. Small colleges have many significant advantages over big universities. There are no simple responses to the question, Which university is best for me? If you attended a small undergraduate college, you may want to attend graduate school at a larger institution. Or, you may be more comfortable remaining at a modest size school, and vice versa. Only you can make that decision.

Some things are fundamental, though. For example, the SSW you attend should have a first-class academic library available to its students, one which subscribes to most of the significant social work journals and has an extensive collection of social work books.

CHARACTERISTICS OF THE LOCAL COMMUNITY

When you choose a school of social work to attend you are also making a decision about what university to attend and where you will live. Each of these three issues can be very important to your life satisfaction and well-being. Although many major colleges and universities provide some form of dormitory life for graduate students, most MSW students choose to live off campus in some form of private housing. Usually campuses are surrounded by student enclaves, which vary tremendously in quality, ranging from sprawling apartment complexes to widows who rent rooms in their antebellum mansions.

The university housing office can provide you with the full range of housing options. Married MSW students, particularly those with children, may find it financially helpful to obtain an apartment in married student or family housing on campus. Family housing is usually connected to the main campus by a bus or shuttle service, which makes owning (and paying for) a car less necessary.

Climate can also factor into your decision. One of the authors, Karen, obtained her PhD in social work in the salubrious climate of Tallahassee, Florida, whereas the other author, Bruce, shivered his way through the winters of Ann Arbor, Michigan. If you like to snow ski, then Colorado may be the place to go to graduate school, but if swimming is more your thing, then give Florida or Hawaii your serious consideration. Like mountain hiking? Try living in Tennessee or West Virginia. It simply makes sense to try to combine your desire to obtain an MSW with living in a place that is attractive to you.

The racial and ethnic composition, as well as other aspects of diversity, of the city and state in which your potential university resides may be important to you. Those uncomfortable in a diverse population may have a difficult time in New York City, whereas gays and lesbians may find it awkward to fit into the social life in some of the more rural college towns. Conversely, a number of metropolitan areas and smaller cities are well known for their friendly and accepting attitude toward gays and lesbians; San Francisco, California, and Northampton, Massachusetts, are but two examples. Members of the Latter Day Saints (Mormons) will find greater understanding of their beliefs by attending graduate school in Utah, whereas devout Roman Catholics may find Catholic University (Washington, D.C.), Boston College, or St. Louis University to be particularly welcoming environments.

Taking the time to pay a visit to your projected SSW/university/town before making your decision about where to attend graduate school is always a good idea. Just as you would be inclined to see the SSW classrooms, look over some of the housing options, tour model apartments, etc. Do not do what one of the authors (Bruce) did—roll into town the day before classes began, with a car laden with clothes and books, drop by the campus housing office, and expect to find idyllic accommodations in half a day. He ended up in a meagerly furnished, albeit expensive, single attic room (cold in the winter and hot in the summer), sharing a lavatory with two other graduate students. No cooking facilities were allowed, only a small refrigerator. There was no TV antenna or cable access, so his only communication with the outside world was a radio, and he had to sign a year-long lease for these palatial surroundings.

By scouting out neighborhoods beforehand, you can have a better idea of possible living arrangements and perhaps obtain a desirable rental some months before the beginning of classes. Do this, of course, *after* being accepted into a given MSW program.

Do take advantage of this opportunity to explore a new place to live. Seattle, Washington; Berkeley, California; New York City; Boston; New Orleans, Louisiana; Austin, Texas; are all exciting, dynamic places to live. Why not go to graduate school in such a city? Of course, big city life may not be for you, which leaves you with a number of very pleasant alternatives—Chapel Hill, North Carolina; Athens, Georgia; Madison, Wisconsin; and Ann Arbor, Michigan.

We asked some of our current MSW students what issues they thought were important in choosing the right MSW program. Here are some of their responses (in no particular order):

> "I think a major factor to be considered in an MSW program is the quality of instructors. This can't be ascertained just by looking at credentials, so I would encourage prospective students to try and contact current students to get the 'low down' on faculty teaching practice and course content, as well as other aspects of the program."

> "Look at the faculty, their areas of interests—are they individuals that will challenge you and be able to support and encourage your focus? How does the faculty relate to the students? Also, when visiting the school, sit in on a class. Experience first hand what it would be like to be a student in that particular MSW program. Assess things such as, did the class hold your interest? Was there a sense of cohesion? Was the class lecture based or discussion based? Depending on your learning style, these items could be very important to your education."

> "It is important to look at the number of students in the program and see if it fits with your comfort level. Also the facilities, such as the building and the comfort of the classrooms. It would also be important to look at faculty and their background, such as a clinical orientation or community organizing, and see how this fits with your own individual interests."

> "Who are the faculty members (i.e., areas of expertise)? Go to the school Web site and find information on the professors and course they teach. Go to the library and read some of the faculty's journal articles. Are your interests congruent with the interests of some of these professors? What are the descriptions of the courses taught? How many courses are students required to complete each term?"

This is an exciting time for you. Pursuing a graduate degree is a major commitment, but it is also a wonderful opportunity to grow professionally and personally. As discussed in this chapter, you will have many variables to consider in selecting those graduate social work

BOX 1   Some Factors to Consider When Choosing an MSW Program

---

Concentrations/training
Types of internships offered
Presence of particular faculty
Class sizes
Competitiveness
Admissions standards (e.g., GRE scores)
Tuition and other costs
Out-of-state schools vs. in-state schools
Advanced standing available?
Part-time study available?
Is distance learning technology used?
Reputation of MSW program
Reputation and comfort of university environment
Livability of surrounding community
Availability of social support networks
Availability of academic resources (e.g., library)

---

programs that are the best fit for you. We urge you to be thoughtful of your personal needs as well as your professional goals and to embrace your search with enthusiasm.

References

Carrillo, D., & Thyer, B. A. (1994). Advanced standing and two-year program MSW students: An empirical investigation of foundation interviewing skills. *Journal of Social Work Education, 30,* 278–288.

Gatz, Y., Patten, S., Thyer, B. A., & Parish, R. T. (1990). Evaluating the effectiveness of a part-time off-campus MSW program. *Journal of Continuing Social Work Education, 5*(2), 11–14.

Ginsberg, L. H. (1998). *Careers in social work.* Boston: Allyn & Bacon.

Ligon, J., Thyer, B. A., & Dixon, D. (1995). Academic affiliations of those published in social work journals: A productivity analysis, 1989–1993. *Journal of Social Work Education, 31,* 251–260.

Morales, A. T., & Sheafor, B. W. (2001). *Social work: A profession of many faces* (9th ed.). Boston: Allyn & Bacon.

National Association of Social Workers. (1993). *Careers in social work* [brochure]. Washington, DC: Author.

National Association of Social Workers. (1997, February). Issuer of degrees pleads to fraud. *NASW News, 42*(2), p 9.

O'Neill, J. V. (1999, June). Profession dominates in mental health. *NASW News, 44*(6), 1, 8.

Peterson's. (1997). *Peterson's graduate programs in business, education, health, information studies, law, & social work.* Princeton, NJ: Peterson's.

Pittman, V. (1997). *Surviving graduate school part time.* Thousand Oaks, CA: Sage.

Thyer, B. A., Artelt, T., Markward, M. K., & Dozier, C. D. (1998). Distance learning in social work education: A replication study. *Journal of Social Work Education, 34,* 291–295.

Thyer, B. A., Polk, G., & Gaudin, J. G. (1997). Distance learning in social work education: A preliminary evaluation. *Journal of Social Work Education, 33,* 363–367.

Thyer, B. A., Vonk, M. E., & Tandy, C. C. (1996). Are advanced standing and two-year MSW program students equivalently prepared? An empirical investigation. *Arete, 20*(2), 42–46.

Chapter 2

WHAT SCHOOLS WANT TO
KNOW AND HOW BEST TO APPLY

Graduate programs in social work are not all alike. It would be much easier on you if all graduate social work programs had the same admission materials, but this just is not the case. Some schools may require an open-ended personal essay, while others may ask you to respond to specific questions. If you will be applying to more than one school, it is very important that you keep your application materials well organized. We know of more than one student who was applying to school X but sent a cover letter with her admission materials to school X with a letter addressed to school Y. This does not impress the school admissions committee. You want to put your best foot forward to impress the school. We hope the following will be useful in your application process.

WHAT ARE THE ADMISSION REQUIREMENTS?

Each SSW bulletin will present something about its admission standards. Among the bits of information you will be required to produce are official transcripts, letters of recommendation, a personal statement about why you wish to earn an MSW, completed application forms (sometimes there are separate ones required for the SSW and graduate school), application fee, and perhaps the results of standardized tests (sent directly from the testing company, at your expense, not from you). The most frequently used standardized test is the Graduate Record Examination (GRE).

Taking the GRE

The GRE is now offered only via computer (with exceptions made for those with disabilities), and the general aptitude test consists of two multiple choice sections and one essay section. There is one verbal section with analogies, reading comprehension, and sentence completions. There is a quantitative section. And there is a section with two essays. Each section is scored separately. Many, but not all, schools of social work require you to submit GRE scores from the general aptitude test. Of those schools which use the GRE as an entrance test, many publish a minimum score that is required for admission. For example, the University of Georgia Graduate School at one time required an applicant to have earned a minimum of 800 on the verbal and quantitative scores combined (the analytic writing subscore is not yet widely used by schools of social work), whereas the College of Social Work at the University of South Carolina does not use the GRE at all.

If the SSW you are interested in requires a GRE score, look at the GRE Web page at www.gre.org to learn more. Your local university career planning center can also help you register for the GRE. Acquire a study guide, take the practice tests, and then take the actual test. If you are genuinely unsure about your ability to do well, consider a formal GRE preparation course offered by any number of private, proprietary firms. Generally though, many people score well on the GRE without one of these courses. Study guides and practice tests are available on CD and online, if you would like to study on your own. Again, the local university career planning center can help you prepare the GRE.

The graduate school you are applying to will instruct you to have the Educational Testing Service (ETS) (the company that produces the GRE) send them an official copy of your score. Most graduate schools will not accept a report form submitted by you.

You can take the GRE as frequently as once per month. If you do not do well the first time, retake it. Most graduate schools will calculate your minimum scores required for entrance into their university by using the best scores among all the repetitions of the GRE you have completed. For example, if you took the GRE in September and scored 550 on the verbal and 425 on the quantitative (for a total of 925) and then took the GRE again in November and scored 535 on the verbal and 510 on the quantitative, the graduate school will take your best verbal score (550 in September) and best quantitative score (510 from

November) for a combined score of 1060. This latter figure would then be the one used as a factor to make an admissions decision on your application.

If you are a poor test taker or simply do badly on the test, take heart. The GRE may not be a particularly good predictor of one's performance in an MSW program (see Donahue & Thyer, 1992), which is why some schools of social work do not use it at all. You should keep in mind that GRE scores are only one of several things being weighed by an admissions committee. Your undergraduate GPA, your personal statement, and your overall fit with the program are extremely important.

Composing the Personal Statement

If your MSW program application asks for a personal statement (and almost all do), take the time to reflect on this assignment carefully, and follow directions exactly. If they request a three-page essay, do not submit a ten-page essay. Take the available space to truthfully describe your career interests, significant events that have led you to consider earning the MSW, what you anticipate being able to contribute to the field, and any populations of clients or areas of practice (e.g., community practice, advocacy, etc.) with which you particularly wish to gain some experience. Admissions committees *do* read your personal statement and will form an immediate impression of you from the statement. Your personal statement is a reflection of you, so pay careful attention to the wording, spelling, and neatness of appearance. Your personal statement should be typed, not handwritten. Ask several trusted colleagues or friends to read your statement and give you constructive feedback.

How Important Is My Undergraduate Grade Point Average?

Once you graduate with your undergraduate degree, your undergraduate GPA is cast in stone and cannot be changed, even if you go back and take additional undergraduate classes. Many students do not understand this. If you have not yet graduated with your undergraduate degree and are not happy with your undergraduate GPA, you may wish to postpone graduation and take some additional courses to raise your GPA. If you have already graduated and have a low GPA, you may wish to take some graduate courses as a non-degree-seeking student to prove that you are capable of successfully undertaking graduate work.

Graduate schools are affected by economic conditions as are most aspects of society. In the mid-to-late 1970s there was a dearth of qualified applicants to MSW programs; in the mid–1980s and early 1990s, there were many, many applicants. Do not let your graduate school plans be swayed by the ups and downs of the economy. Forge ahead in earning your MSW.

Your overall grade point average (GPA) is a crucial element used by admissions offices in making a decision about your admission. Many of the elite schools of social work require quite high GPAs, so if yours is quite low, do not write off applying to the elite schools, but realize that you will need to be extra strong in other aspects (like very high GRE scores, a knockout personal statement, or glowing letters of recommendation).

Obtaining Letters of Reference

Many graduate schools of social work require three to five letters of reference. If required, this will be clearly stated in the instruction sheet on how to apply. Read this carefully. Some schools stipulate that persons serving as a reference must have known you for a certain period of time, or they may require a certain number of work references and a certain number of personal references. Whatever the stipulation, make certain that you choose your references carefully. Ideally, your reference should know you and be willing to write you a good letter of reference. You should always contact your reference far enough in advance of the deadline for him or her to not be rushed when writing the letter. You may also want to ask them if they feel comfortable providing you with a good reference. Obtain letters of reference/recommendation from professional people who know you well and can comment on your ability to successfully undertake graduate-level work. An honest letter from someone who knows you well will serve you better than a glowing statement high on superlatives but low on concrete facts written by a high-ranking public official with whom you or your family are minimally acquainted. Providing your letter writer with information about the schools to which you plan to apply, your GPA and GRE scores, your career goals, and your work experience (a resume may be helpful), and if applicable, your undergraduate field experiences, will be very helpful to them in composing the letter of reference. The more information you provide them, the easier it will be for them to provide a full and accurate reference. If the graduate social work programs provide specific forms to be used for the reference, make sure that your reference person understands this and provide them with copies of the form. If you have been out of school for a while or out of contact with your previous professors, do not despair. Most undergraduate programs retain complete files on alumni, and once you speak with a past faculty member, chances are that he or she will remember you. However, all the more reason to provide your reference with lots of current information about you. Most graduate schools appreciate having applicants who have "life" and "work" experience, so you should not view a gap in time between your undergraduate degree and application to a graduate program as a deficit. Indeed, we often find that our older, more experienced students earn higher grades and get more out of the graduate school experience.

If the university uses a printed recommendation form and you are asked to indicate whether or not the recommendation may be considered confidential (i.e., you give up the right to have subsequent access to the letter), this sends the message that the letter may be more honestly written than one wherein the person providing the recommendation knows that you may see the letter later.

If you are asked to supply three letters of reference, you might want to consider asking five individuals. This will ensure that the graduate admissions office receives at least three. Your application will be held as incomplete until the minimum number of reference letters are received. Chances are that more than the minimal number will not hurt you, but less will certainly delay the processing of your application.

The Interview

Some graduate schools of social work require an interview. Should you be asked or required to undergo an interview, we suggest that you view this as an opportunity to impress the admissions committee. This is the time when you can augment your application materials with your personal self. This is a time to put your best foot forward: Be on time (start out early—parking at colleges/universities can be tricky) and dress appropriately (we suggest business casual attire). Review all your application materials again before the interview so that your responses to the interviewers are consistent with your written materials. Be prepared to discuss your reasons for wanting to go to graduate school, your desire to enter the profession of social work, your career aspirations, and your eagerness to work hard and excel in the program. When you first meet with the interviewers, shake their hands and look them in the eye. Mention how pleased you are to meet them. When the interview is over, shake hands with them again and thank them for the interview. After you return home, you should follow up with a note to the interviewers thanking them for the interview and reiterating your interest in their graduate program.

OBTAINING FINANCIAL ASSISTANCE

Financial support for graduate school is an important consideration. Graduate social work education can be expensive, but financial assistance is available. Financial planning requires knowledge of the sources of financial assistance, application procedures, and deadlines. Your public library and college financial aid office are good sources of information on financial assistance. You should also check out the U.S. Department of Education Web site Financial Aid for Students home page at http://www.ed.gov/finaid.html for information about grants, loans, work study, and tax credits for education and how to apply for them. You can fill out a free application for federal student aid quickly and easily right on the Web.

Most colleges and universities have two basic forms of aid: merit-based awards (typically in the form of scholarships, fellowships, research and teaching assistantships) and grants and loans that require that the student pay back the money borrowed. Federal and state regulations related to loans and grants change frequently, so it is important to access current information. Sources of financial assistance usually include federal and state government funds, grants and scholarships, and loans. Most colleges and universities have financial assistance in the form of assistantships, fellowships, employment, and loans. The graduate school or office of graduate studies at your college or university can provide you with information on all the types of financial assistance available. You may also find this information on your university's Web site.

You can increase your chances of receiving the best need-based loans or grants from the office of financial aid if you apply early and fill out the forms carefully. To receive financial assistance an applicant often must meet eligibility requirements. Factors that determine eligibility include admission and enrollment status, school accreditation, and your student status. Some federal and state aid packages require that a student be enrolled for a minimum of half-time study. Half-time study is often defined differently by schools using semester hours, credit hours, clock hours, or trimester and quarter systems. Proof of satisfactory academic progress may be required to maintain eligibility after the first year. An institution must be nationally accredited for students to qualify for federal or state aid. Financial assistance programs define students as dependent or independent. Dependent students rely at least partially on their parents for financial support. Independent students do not rely on parents for financial support.

Federal regulations state that a student classified as independent must fit one of the following categories:

be of age 24 by December 31 of the award year;

be an orphan, ward of the court, or veteran of the armed services;

have legal dependents other than a spouse;

be married, a professional student, or a graduate student, and not be claimed as a dependent for tax purposes by a parent for the first year of the award year;

be a single undergraduate, under age 24, with no dependents, and not be claimed as a dependent for tax purposes by a parent for either of the two calendar years preceding the award year; demonstrate self-sufficiency by showing an income of at least $4,000 in each of those two years; or

be judged independent by the financial aid officer (FAO), based on documented circumstances.

Institutional Loans

Before an institution considers a request for financial assistance, it determines how much the applicant can afford to pay; this is called a needs analysis. The needs analysis is performed by the College Board's College Scholarship Service or the American College Testing Program. Both services determine how much the student can be expected to pay. If the amount the student is expected to contribute is less than the cost of attending the institution of choice, the student is determined to have financial need. The FAO plays a major role in determining eligibility for and amount of financial assistance. For instance, the FAO can increase or decrease the amount of family contribution identified by the needs analysis, can allocate money controlled by the institution or certify the student's eligibility for money from other sources, and determines the percentage of loans, grants, and scholarships that make up the total financial assistance package.

Student Loans

Federal loans. The federal government offers low-interest loans to assist students with college expenses. Interest on some loans is paid by the government while the student is enrolled in school. The government may guarantee the loan against default. In some instances the loan may be deferred or canceled in exchange for public service work. A six- to nine-month grace period after graduation may be granted before repayment of the loan begins. For more information visit the U.S. Department of Education Student Financial Assistance Web page at http://www.ed.gov/finaid.html. This Web site provides information about grants, loans, work-study, and tax credits for education and how to apply for them. You can fill out the Free Application for Federal Student Aid (FAFSA) quickly and easily on the Web. If you are filing a paper application, you can use the Federal (Title IV) School Code Search on the Web to look up the codes for the colleges that you are considering so that you can list them on the FAFSA.

Stafford Loans. Stafford Loans are low-interest loans for undergraduate and graduate students who are U.S. citizens or resident aliens and who are enrolled at least half-time, regardless of need. The lenders for these loans are banks, savings and loan associations, insurance companies, and credit unions. There are basically two types of loans: subsidized and unsubsidized loans. Subsidized loans are need-based. With a subsidized loan, the federal government pays the interest while the student is enrolled in school. The borrower of the subsidized loan pays a 5 percent origination fee that is deducted proportionately from each loan disbursement. Unsubsidized loans are non–need based, and the borrower is responsible for paying interest during enrollment. Generally, graduate students can borrow up to $18,500 each academic year, although only $8,500 of this amount may be in subsidized Stafford Loans. You may receive less than the yearly maximum amount if you receive other financial aid that is used to cover a portion of your cost of attendance at graduate school. Borrowers of unsubsidized loans pay an origination fee that is deducted proportionately from each loan disbursement. You must be attending an accredited college or university to be eligible for the Federal Stafford Loan Program. Your loan money must first be used to pay for your tuition and fees, room and board, and other school charges. If loan money remains, you will receive the funds by check or in cash unless you give the school written permission to hold the funds until later in the enrollment period.

Supplemental Loans to Students. The Supplemental Loans to Students (SLS) program is restricted to professional students, graduate students, and independent undergraduate students. SLS applicants must apply for Stafford Loans before being considered for SLS. Lenders are banks, savings and loan associations, credit unions, and insurance companies. Interest rates are adjusted annually, and interest accrues during all periods of the loan, including deferments. Repayment of the principal and interest begins within sixty days after the final disbursement. SLS borrowers who also have Federal Stafford Loans can begin repayment on both loans at the same time (six months after leaving school or dropping below half-time enrollment). The lender must offer the option of "income-sensitive repayment," which means that an individual's financial situation is taken into account when determining the monthly payment.

Federal Perkins Loans. Federal Perkins Loans are administered by colleges and universities for undergraduate and graduate students with exceptional financial need. The loan funds are allocated to schools by the federal government. Your school is your lender. The loan is made with government funds with a share contributed by the school. You must repay this loan to your school. Depending on when you apply, your level of need, and the funding level of the school, you can borrow up to $6,000 for each year of graduate or professional study. The total amount you can borrow as a graduate/professional student is $40,000. This amount includes any Perkins Loans you borrowed as an undergraduate. The borrower does not pay interest while attending school, during deferments, or during the grace period that follows each deferment. Generous deferment policies apply for volunteers in the Peace Corps, Service to America, and other similar public service organizations, as well as for students in internships, students on parental leave, and working mothers. Loans may be repaid by the federal government in exchange for service in the National Guard or military reserve and for active military duty personnel. A nine-month grace period after graduation is granted before repayment begins. Perkins Loans are not equally available at all schools. The amount allotted to a school depends on its student default rate for repayment. The maximum annual loan amount is $6,000 for graduate students. Perkins Loans go to students with the greatest financial need, and there are relatively few funds available, so apply early.

Federal work study. Federal work study provides jobs for undergraduate and graduate students who need financial assistance. Federal funds are made available to participating colleges and universities. Jobs are awarded as part of financial assistance packages. Under this need-based program, the government pays up to 75 percent of your wages and the employer provides the remainder. The student receives money from the fund in addition to the wages from the job. The pay level is at least current federal minimum wage. Jobs are usually on campus working for the school or off campus with a nonprofit organization or state or federal agency. The amount you earn cannot exceed your total federal work-study award. The work schedule is set by the school.

State programs. States contribute relatively little to graduate education compared with the federal government, only 3 percent of total aid. This aid is usually only for state residents attending school within the state. State aid programs include grants, tuition assistance, fee reductions, and loans. Some states have reciprocal agreements that allow students from one state to attend college in another state at reduced tuition. Special programs usually exist for minority students, veterans, National Guard members, and military dependents. Many states give merit awards or scholarships for outstanding academic achievement or exceptionally high scores on the Graduate Record Examination.

Private funding programs. Support to attend graduate school is also available from private sources. All education institutions have endowments for scholarship aid and make these awards independently. They are generally awarded for academic excellence and are not based on financial need. Corporations may establish scholarships for children of employees and retirees. Civic and fraternal organizations may offer scholarships for local students. Private foundation funds are also available, usually for graduate and doctoral students. You can start researching these sources by asking for the appropriate publications at your library or financial aid office.

Be aware that there are many scam artists offering scholarships in exchange for application fees that may exceed $100. Every year, several hundred thousand students and parents are defrauded by scholarship scams. Scam operations often imitate legitimate government agencies, grant-giving foundations, education lenders, and scholarship matching services. Legitimate nonprofits that offer scholarships do not charge fees. In general, you should be wary of scholarships with an application fee. Scholarship matching services that guarantee success, advance-fee loan scams, and sales pitches disguised as financial aid seminars may not be legitimate. For more information on how to avoid scholarship scams, visit http://www.finaid.org/scholarships/scams.phtml.

Tuition aid from employers. Many corporations, state agencies, and other employers offer full or partial tuition reimbursement for employees. Reimbursement may be a free benefit or may require repayment in the form of employment at the institution for a specified number of years. Most tuition reimbursement programs require that courses be job-related. Most employers require a specified length of employment before eligibility for reimbursement begins.

SURVIVAL STRATEGIES

- Obtain a reasonably comprehensive, current book on financial assistance. The public library and college financial aid offices are good resources of information on financial assistance.
- Use college catalogs to learn about financial assistance offered by the school. Ask an admissions advisor or the financial aid office about details.
- Start figuring out your finances at least a year ahead of time, if possible.
- Apply for financial assistance early. Ideally, have your applications in the mail on January 2, the earliest date at which federal law allows submission. Your chance of getting grants or low-interest loans depends in part on whether there is still money in the pot when you apply. So, the earlier the better.
- Be careful in filling out your financial aid forms, because a mistake may cause the form to be rejected and a delay can cause you to lose out on limited aid.
- Present your financial need as strongly as legally possible for the needs analysis.
- Investigate student loans available through banks and savings and loan associations.
- Apply to all major assistance programs.
- Apply for assistance early, and complete all forms thoroughly to avoid delays in processing.
- Check with the financial aid office or dean about scholarships or grants available.
- If already employed, investigate employer's tuition reimbursement programs. Determine the eligibility terms and any commitments required in return for participation in the program.
- If lack of money threatens your continued study, discuss the situation with the financial aid officer. Emergency assistance is commonly available to help meet extraordinary needs.
- If financial assistance is contingent on satisfactory academic achievement, you may want to consider beginning with a light course load to avoid risking loss of assistance.

Self-Funding

Many graduate students work at part- or full-time jobs, perhaps unrelated to the field of social work. Many other students work part-time during the school year and full-time during the summer. Consider these options in lieu of having to drop out of school. One of the authors worked full-time during the evening shift as a technician on the psychiatric ward of the local general hospital. This lasted about ten months and, while very grueling, made it possible to remain in school. Most local college or university communities have plenty of unskilled and semiskilled openings year round—waiting tables is one option. Be creative. For example, we know of one family who needs a roommate for their intellectually disabled twenty-year-old son (he lives in his own home). The roommate is paid about $24,000 per year and is expected to be in the home from 5:00 p.m. to 9:00 a.m., Monday through Friday. For the weekends they have hired another care provider who stays with their son from 5:00 p.m. on Friday to 9:00 a.m. on Monday, and this person earns about $170 per weekend. These are but two examples of the types of nontraditional jobs one can engage in while a graduate student.

Another possibility is to register with a temporary employment agency—interview with them, take a typing test, list any computer or office skills you have (e.g., using word processing or various spreadsheet programs), and indicate when you are available to work. You could work on weekends, or one day a week when you are not in classes. They will call you when suitable openings occur, and you may choose whether or not to take the job that given day. This can be a flexible way to earn $50 to $75 a day while a graduate student. They also may often have openings for simple laborers to do things like help an elderly couple with a yard project or home painting.

Using the above information, instructions, and hints, begin learning about potential MSW programs you would like to attend. Carefully weigh the features of the school itself, the university, and the surrounding community to decide on viable programs to apply to. Apply to several programs, including some of the very best ones you could imagine attending, irrespective of tuition costs. Maybe have a backup school, one of the second- or third-tier institutions to which you think you have a very good chance of being accepted. Once accepted, apply for and see what type of financial assistance is forthcoming. Then, and only then, as your letters of acceptance come rolling in, are you faced with the decision about where to go. Some schools will ask you for an early commitment, maybe even a tuition deposit, to hold your place. You may find yourself in a dilemma—should you confirm your acceptance to State University, since they have accepted you and asked for a confirmation within three weeks, or hold off confirming (and maybe lose your place at State University) while you wait to hear from Ivory Tower University? It is not a good practice to confirm at State University and then when Ivory Tower University accepts you, to then decline State University, perhaps only a few weeks before their classes begin. But if you do decide to attend someplace else, be courteous and give the admissions office at the first school ample time to find a replacement for you from their waiting list.

Good luck in your choices and in your application process.

References

Donahue, B., & Thyer, B. A. (1992). Should the GRE be used as an admissions requirement by schools of social work? *Journal of Teaching in Social Work, 6*(2), 33–40.

Chapter 3

STRATEGIES FOR SUPPORT
AND SURVIVAL

ESTABLISHING AND MAINTAINING SUPPORT SYSTEMS

Graduate school can be demanding and stressful. Establishing and maintaining good support systems can be critical to your success. Prepare your family and friends ahead of time for the demands that will be made on you during graduate school. Ask for their help and support. Attempt to temporarily delegate some of your household or outside responsibilities to others. If you plan to work while you are attending school, speak with your supervisor about the possibility of working more flexible hours, reducing your work hours, or using your vacation time to support time you will need to devote to your graduate studies.

Create a comfortable, quiet environment within your home for studying. The study environment should influence your ability to concentrate on and learn new material. Keep this area free from distractions such as the radio, television, and phone. Your study environment should be clearly labeled as off limits to those who are not studying. Most colleges and universities have an office that provides support to adult students who may have been out of the academic environment for a time. Services provided usually include academic advising, peer support programs, orientation programs, information about financial aid, and educational workshops. These support services can be extremely useful if you need help or support in study skills, time management, or in locating financial support.

SURVIVAL STRATEGIES

- Prepare friends and family for your commitment to graduate school.

- Temporarily delegate responsibilities to others.
- Create a comfortable, quiet work environment.
- Locate the office for adult student services on your campus. Call to make an appointment to find out what services they offer that may be helpful to you during your course of study.

SETTING REALISTIC GOALS

Upon your acceptance into a graduate social work program, you will most probably be assigned a faculty advisor. Meet with your faculty advisor early on. It is important that you share your goals and objectives with your advisor. Your advisor can help you establish a realistic course load given your other family and work responsibilities. Develop a plan of study with your advisor from beginning the program to graduating. It is important that you discuss the number of courses you will take per semester and the amount of time you will need to allocate for field placement. Your faculty advisor can help you select the amount of courses and potential placements that will best fit your unique situation. If you are working and/or have family responsibilities, you will need to find flexibility in your schedule to accommodate required courses and field placement. Although many programs offer part-time course work and extended hours for field placements, it is not realistic to assume that any program will fit your schedule perfectly.

Success in graduate school depends on successful study skills and management of time. It also depends on your attitude toward learning. You will need to develop a positive attitude toward studying and learning. Being enthusiastic and viewing learning as a challenge will help keep you focused and on task. If you set and meet deadlines you will become goal-directed and more efficient. Reward your successful completion of tasks. Plan long-term rewards for completing long or difficult assignments.

If you find that you are having difficulty studying or with a particular subject, do not wait until it is too late. Seek help from instructors and tutors right away. Becoming a member of a study group can be enormously helpful in keeping on track with your coursework. Many students who study in groups perform better than if they had studied alone. Because almost all graduate social work programs have fairly rigid course prerequisites, it is extremely important that you successfully complete your course work to remain on track. Failing or dropping a course could cause you to postpone graduation by as much as a year.

SURVIVAL STRATEGIES

- Meet with your faculty advisor. Discuss your outside responsibilities and ask for his or her help in setting up a realistic schedule of course work.
- Find out what resources exist for special help and tutoring, should they become necessary.
- Consider forming a study group or joining a study group.

TIME MANAGEMENT

Time management is the efficient use of time to meet all obligations and achieve specific objectives. The way you use your time will influence your ability to prepare for classes, complete assignments, and review for examinations. The days when teachers looked over your shoulder and nagged you about assignments and tests are gone. In many classes, especially at larger schools, instructors will not tolerate late assignments or missed exams. In graduate school, instructors assume you are sufficiently responsible to keep up with your work without individual attention. Most graduate school instructors evaluate students solely on the basis of two or three assessments—for most, probably a midterm, final, term project, or several papers. Reading assignments will be longer and less structured than in an undergraduate program. For example, instead of saying, "Read these ten pages for tomorrow," the professor will tell you, "Read this book before the next midterm." Just as often, the professor will not say anything about assignments but rely on the syllabus given to each student the first day of class. With class work structured in this way, falling behind tends to haunt anyone with the slightest inclination toward procrastination. Those who successfully employed cramming as a primary study method as an undergraduate will find this method a surefire means to failure in graduate school.

If you are like so many other students nowadays, you may have many obligations beyond school. These may include family, employment, social, and other obligations. Needless to say, time management plays a large role in any successful graduate school career. Managing your time well requires that you identify your multiple obligations, set priorities, estimate the time needed for tasks associated with your priorities, and develop a realistic and workable schedule.

Establishing priorities is the first step toward effective time management. Setting priorities requires that you identify obligations and rank them according to their level of importance.

SURVIVAL STRATEGIES

- List all of your highest priority activities such as work, meal preparation, children's lessons, appointments, and classes to identify regular obligations.
- List secondary activities such as volunteer work, social events, and entertaining.
- Prioritize items of each list. Decide which activities are essential and which can be postponed, eliminated, or delegated to others.
- Recruit others for tasks that do not require your personal attention.

Once you have established your priorities, you should estimate the time involved for your highest priorities such as study, work, and home commitments. This will require that you be realistic. You should consider your abilities and past experience when allotting time for school and study. The general rule for calculating study time for graduate school is three hours of study for each hour of class. Of course, the actual time you will need for study will vary according to the difficulty of the subject, your prior knowledge of the subject, and your personal interest in the subject. You should set specific hours to keep up with course assignments, learn new material, and review old material. Many students try to play catch-up all year. You have undoubtedly played this game yourself: the professor explains one section, and you read it two weeks later. This is not a productive use of time. By reading the assignments before class, the lecture material will be clearer and easier to absorb. Most graduate professors have an expectation that students come to class prepared, and this expectation includes having read the assigned readings for the class period. Because you are going to have to read the material anyway, you will be best served by being prepared for each class session. For most students, some study each day is more productive and improves retention and recall more than one or two full days of intermittent study does. You will learn more efficiently when your study time is planned and you study at your peak performance times. Remember to be realistic when planning your study time. Fatigue interferes with learning. Studies indicate that studying fifty to sixty minutes followed by a fifteen-minute break is the best for most learners.

Class attendance must be a high priority on your time-management schedule. Graduate social work classes often include modules associated with skill development and experiential learning exercises as well as lecture. Graduate professors assume students are disciplined enough to attend class on a regular basis. Because of the experiential nature of many of the classes, attendance and class participation may play a big role in the course grade. Whether or not this is the case, class attendance is critical to graduate school success.

SURVIVAL STRATEGIES

- Analyze your priorities and assignments. Assign sufficient time for each task. Allow extra time for projects or assignments that might be difficult or require large amounts of time in the library or reading outside research.
- Plan time for textbook reading to keep up with course material.
- Plan time for outside readings and research.
- Plan time for typing, word processing, and photocopying.
- Plan time to prepare written assignments such as papers or journals.
- Plan time to prepare group presentations, projects, and oral reports.
- Plan time for travel to school and field placement sites.

SCHEDULING

Keeping a time-management schedule will be critical to you being successful in graduate school and reducing unnecessary stress. Your schedule should reflect your priorities, with the most important activities accorded the most time. It should show the time estimated for each task, including family, work, and social commitments as well as school assignments, tests, and study periods. A schedule should be realistic, goal oriented, and should allow for unexpected variables. In establishing your schedule, try to plan to study when interruption is least likely so that you can maintain your attention and concentration. Provide sufficient time in your schedule to read your lecture notes from class at the end of each day or at least the end of the week. Students who do this find they do not have to study as much right before final exams because the material already has been planted firmly in their minds. It is often useful to start each study period with the most difficult subject or task to be as alert as possible. If you must study when you are tired, choose subjects that require the least concentration.

SURVIVAL STRATEGIES

- Use a large calendar to plan the entire semester; use smaller monthly or weekly calendars for specific activities.
- Record all firmly committed periods such as class, laboratory, and field placement times.
- Record examination dates and due dates for assignments.
- Record employment and social obligations.
- Identify free periods of time.
- Schedule school and home study time during free periods. Alert family members and friends to at-home study times to avoid interruptions.
- Use time between classes for review, preparation, and library use.
- Be flexible; a week or two into the semester, adjust the schedule as necessary.
- Schedule extra time for difficult subjects; do not steal time from one subject to work on another.

- When overwhelmed, falling behind, or physically exhausted, review the schedule and seek advice from an academic counselor.
- Schedule your study time for your peak performance times.
- Schedule frequent short study periods rather than occasional long sessions for easier incorporation into a daily routine.
- Schedule study time for each day.
- Schedule time for rest and relaxation to avoid overwork and stress.

Good organizational and time management skills can make the difference in your ability to be successful in graduate school. The time and work commitments may seem overwhelming. Putting a plan in place *at the beginning* of each semester will help to keep you from becoming overwhelmed and discouraged. And remember, despite all the hard work and challenges, your graduate studies are time limited. The fruits of your labors will be well worth the effort when you graduate and find a rewarding position as a graduate-level social worker.

Chapter 4

GETTING STARTED IN GRADUATE SCHOOL

A new school can be exciting and challenging, but it also can be confusing and frightening. Graduate school can be overwhelming because of its size, complexity, and the unfamiliarity of new surroundings. Preparing yourself for this new experience can help ease your entrance into the new program, reduce some of your anxiety, and save you time and energy that you will undoubtedly need as you embark on this new adventure.

You can prepare for matriculation into a graduate social work program ahead of time by (1) obtaining support from family or friends to minimize or avoid conflicts; (2) becoming familiar with the layout of the school and campus; (3) finding a suitable place to live; (4) preparing for registration and matriculation to avoid errors; (5) becoming familiar with the school and university/college services; (6) becoming familiar with the school and university/college procedures, regulations, and protocols; and (7) becoming familiar with student organizations.

OBTAINING SUPPORT FROM FAMILY AND FRIENDS TO MINIMIZE OR AVOID CONFLICTS

Graduate school can be very demanding physically, emotionally, and intellectually. Countless students enter graduate school unprepared for the challenges ahead. Preparing yourself, your family, and your friends ahead of time can help prevent conflicts and problems from occurring. If you will be moving to attend graduate school, you will need to either cope with separation from family and friends and/or help prepare your partner and children for the move. Helping to prepare your family and friends for the expected changes in your life is critical. Time management and reallocation of responsibilities within the family should be discussed and agreed on before starting the program. Equally important is the emotional support that friends and family can provide to you while these new changes take place in your life.

SURVIVAL STRATEGIES

- The amount of support you will require is, of course, dependent on your own personal traits and circumstances. However, most people entering a new and challenging phase in their life can benefit from the support and caring of close friends and family. We suggest that you discuss your goals, anticipated time commitments, and expected demands of the social work graduate program with your family and friends. This will help prepare you and them for the demands ahead.
- As much as possible, try to involve your partner, children, and extended family members in the planning and decision making.
- If you are moving with your family, you should discuss daily routines and responsibilities such as cooking, housecleaning, child care, transportation, and extracurricular commitments to identify any potential problems or conflicts.
- If you will be moving away from family, you will need to discuss the ways in which you can maintain communication and relationships, the time you will have available to spend with them (perhaps over holidays), and how they can be helpful and supportive to you while you are in the program.
- Whether your family will be with you or at a distance, you should prepare them for the amount of time you will need to devote to study and assignments.
- Preparing family and friends for the amount of private quiet time you will need to fulfill the academic and professional demands of social work graduate education will help to prevent hurt feelings.
- Graduate social work programs often encourage teamwork in classroom assignments and study groups among the students. This practice is a wonderful way of making new friends and

establishing an additional support for yourself while in the program. Spouses and partners need to be reassured by you that these activities are not threatening to your relationship with them.

BECOMING FAMILIAR WITH THE LAYOUT OF THE SCHOOL AND CAMPUS

A graduate school of social work may be part of a large, sprawling campus or on a small campus of just a few buildings. Typically, a graduate school of social work is housed in one building surrounded by other academic buildings (nursing, engineering, architecture, etc.). Familiarizing yourself with the layout of the campus and buildings, bus routes, and parking can help alleviate fear of getting lost and being late for class. You will need to be able to locate the administrative and faculty offices of the school of social work, buildings where classes are held, the library, the bursar's office, the office of financial aid, bookstore, cafeteria, the office of student services, and the student medical clinic. You should also attempt to locate where you can obtain photocopying services.

SURVIVAL STRATEGIES

- A campus directory and map depicting the layout of the campus may be contained in the university or college bulletin or catalog. If one is not, contact the office of student services and request a campus map, or, if the university or college has a Web site, you may be able to download a copy of the campus map and print it from your own computer.
- Many colleges and universities have virtual walking tours of the campus through their Web site. This is also an excellent way to familiarize yourself with the campus before you get there.
- It is also helpful to familiarize yourself with the area surrounding the university. Contact the local chamber of commerce for information regarding the surrounding city or town. They will often supply you with maps, information regarding housing,

public transportation, parks and recreation, as well as employment information. Most cities and towns now have Web sites that you can visit to obtain a plethora of information about the surrounding area.

- If at all possible, visit the campus and school of social work prior to beginning classes. Many social work programs welcome a visit from prospective and admitted students and will schedule meetings for you ahead of time to find out about registration and other details.

- You may wish to meet with other students already in the program and with some faculty in your area of interest. Some programs will provide you with a walking tour and orientation, while other programs do little of this. Find out ahead of time what kind of introduction to the program, campus, and surrounding area you can expect, and then be prepared to augment this with your own information gathering, fact finding, and familiarization.

- We suggest that you plan to move well in advance of the first day of classes. Moving to a new residence can take some adjustment. Being completely moved in, settled, and set up prior to the start of the program will give you the opportunity to become acclimated to your new surroundings and to investigate the campus and local area.

FINDING A SUITABLE PLACE TO LIVE

Most colleges and universities have on-campus housing for married or unmarried graduate students and can be helpful to you in finding off-campus housing alternatives. Given your personal circumstances, you need to think carefully about the most appropriate housing accommodations for you. Graduate on-campus student housing may provide you with easy access to classes and the library as well as student organization and university activities, saving you time and expense for transportation and parking. Some graduate housing is less expensive than housing off campus and may be more affordable, while other graduate housing may be just as expensive as living off campus.

47

SURVIVAL STRATEGIES

- Contact the university's housing office well in advance of your anticipated move date. Most universities or colleges can provide you with information regarding on-campus graduate housing and off-campus housing possibilities.
- Check the university's student bulletin board Web site, where housing availability, room availability, and roommate options are often posted. Most cities now also have Web sites that have apartment and housing rental information. Do not put off your housing investigation. Housing options become fewer (and more costly) as the new academic year approaches. Graduate student housing is often at a premium and requires an early deposit to hold your space.

REGISTERING AND MATRICULATING

After you have been admitted to the social work program you will probably receive a copy of the university catalog, the social work program bulletin listing course offerings, information regarding fees and financial aid, and a copy of the student handbook. If you do not receive all these materials, contact the school well in advance of your matriculation to obtain them. These materials are critical to your success in graduate school. Most universities consider the institution's academic catalog to be a type of contract between the student and the institution. Read the catalog carefully. Countless numbers of students have delayed their graduation because they did not thoroughly inform themselves of the course requirements, timing of course offerings, prerequisites and corequisites of courses, and program standards for remaining in good standing as a student. Read all material thoroughly, and keep the material close by for easy access and reference. Do not rely on fellow students for guidance regarding course registration or questions regarding the program. Faulty information is often passed among students, and as in any organization, rumors can take on lives of their own. Always consult the official university and school documents to provide you with guidance. If you are still in doubt, meet with your faculty advisor or an official of the school of social work for guidance.

Most graduate schools of social work offer orientation for new students. Not all schools have the same type of orientation. Some may be one day while others may be several days. Some might be during the middle of summer or right before schools starts. Orientation activities will be different at each school. It is important that you participate in orientation. Most schools use orientation as a means to provide new students with important information, introduce them to the library and computer lab, and assist them in registration for classes. Orientation is also an opportunity for you to meet new friends and potential study mates. Remember, everyone at orientation is in the same boat— a new environment, a new group of people, a new school—and everyone will be as eager to meet you as you are to meet them.

Most colleges and universities require that a student be admitted by the graduate school of social work and the dean of graduate studies of the university. Generally, registration must reflect courses taken for graduate credit, and the course must be approved by the graduate council of the university and by the academic advisor in the school of social work.

Registration is the official enrollment in courses and usually occurs prior to or during the first few days of a semester. All courses offered in a semester, along with day, time, and location of class and credit hours given, are listed in a catalog or bulletin. You will select classes according to the graduate school guidelines and program requirements. Make sure that you meet with your academic advisor for advising before registering for courses.

It is a good idea to find out where and how registration is conducted. Many programs offer registration online. You may wish to speak with some advanced students or your academic advisor regarding specific registration procedures. Most programs require that you complete a university schedule form, and in some cases, this must be signed by your academic advisor. In addition, you may be required to show proof of in-state residency, health records indicating inoculations, and other required materials. Consult the university catalog, your academic advisor, and experienced students before registration.

SURVIVAL STRATEGIES

- Obtain copies of the university or college catalog and the school of social work bulletin. Browse the university and school of social work Web sites. Pay careful attention to all instructions.

- You may be required to advise the school of your intent to enter the program and may also be required to submit a fee to hold your space. Failing to advise the school of your intent to enroll or to pay a "sitting fee" may disqualify you from admission, and another student will be given the opportunity to take your place.
- Attend the scheduled orientation. Participate in as many activities as possible. Make a real effort to meet as many of your new fellow classmates as possible. Introduce yourself to faculty.
- Student advising and registration dates are generally taken very seriously by graduate social work programs. Because registration and course selection can be somewhat overwhelming, it is a good idea to discuss course selection with your faculty advisor ahead of time.
- Know the course requirements and course sequence before registration. Have your school bulletin and catalog handy.
- Because most programs cap the number of students allowed in each section of each class, early advising and registration will enhance your chances of getting the classes you want.
- Make certain that you have all required forms and papers with you before arriving for registration (or submitted in advance if you are registering online). If you are not prepared with the proper documentation, you will probably be refused registration until you can produce these documents.
- You should be prepared to pay for your tuition or show evidence of waiver from the financial aid office at the time of registration. You will not be able to register without payment or a waiver.

Scheduling Classes

You will need to check the university catalog or bulletin for the schedule of classes. The schedule bulletin should contain a listing of all courses being offered for a specific term. Check the schedule early. Most graduate programs offer only the exact amount of course sections to meet student needs. The earlier you register, the more likely it is that you will be able to get the courses that fit with your desired schedule. However, you should be prepared to be flexible with your own schedule in order to fit in required courses.

SURVIVAL STRATEGIES

- Consult with your academic advisor in selecting your course of study.
- Consult the schedule bulletin, and prepare a list of preferred course times.
- Prepare an alternate schedule in case your first-preference selection is already filled.

The Importance of Prerequisites and Corequisites

Most graduate social work programs have fairly rigid prerequisites and corequisite course requirements. Prerequisite means that you must have successfully completed a certain course before you can register for a specific course. Corequisite means that two or more courses must be taken at the same time. The graduate social work curriculum is one that is built on building blocks of knowledge. A graduate social work program that has been accredited by the Council on Social Work Education will have a set curriculum that it follows. The accreditation is granted on the basis of the curriculum that the social work program has prescribed to the Council on Social Work Education. This accreditation assumes that the social work program will adhere to its curriculum as proposed to the Council, including sequencing of courses and observance of prerequisites and corequisites. As a result, you will be required to take and successfully complete certain aspects of the curriculum before proceeding further in the program. Most graduate social work programs follow the prescribed course of studies very closely. Some student have difficulty understanding the importance of following the prescribed course of studies and are often surprised at the inflexibility of the graduate social work program. However, allowing students to stray from the prescribed course of studies can put a graduate social work program in a difficult situation with the accrediting agency. You certainly want to graduate from an accredited social work program and would not want to place your program at risk of loss of accreditation.

SURVIVAL STRATEGIES

- Read the college catalog and student handbook thoroughly.
- Pay careful attention to course sequencing requirements.

- Meet with your faculty advisor for expert assistance in making certain that you are taking courses in the proper sequence.

Tuition and Fees

University fees and other charges are determined by each institution and are usually subject to change without notice. At most institutions, all student fees are due in advance unless you have been granted a waiver. If your tuition is prepaid or waived, most institutions still require that you confirm your attendance by either making a minimum holding payment or signing a confirmation of attendance form. If you do not pay your tuition or complete the attendance form, chances are that your classes will be canceled. Reinstatement of classes generally is accompanied by a late fee. In addition to a late fee, cancellation of classes may cause you to be closed out of the courses for which you originally registered.

At most institutions, students are mailed statements that include their class schedule, drop/add instructions, current tuition and fees, fee waiver information, fines and past-due amounts, pending financial aid that can be credited toward the accounts, any excess funds from scholarships and/or loans, and choices about how to receive them. Often, students who register and pay early receive a reduction in tuition if the payment deadlines are observed.

In addition to tuition, you can expect to pay university program and services fees. These fees may cover non-instructional facilities and programs of an educational, cultural, social, recreational, and service nature; a student health fee; a technology fee; and other miscellaneous fees. Some social work programs require that students pay a fee to cover malpractice insurance while in field practicum. If you are planning to live on campus in graduate student housing, you should expect to pay for a year or semester in advance, although some institutions allow you to pay in monthly installments.

SURVIVAL STRATEGIES

- Consult the university catalog for tuition and fee requirements.
- Consult the social work program student handbook for fees associated with the graduate social work program.

- If you are receiving a loan, grant, scholarship, or another form of tuition waiver, make certain that you have the appropriate paperwork on file with the registrar and bursar's office.
- Pay your tuition and fees on time to avoid being dropped from your classes and being assessed a late fee or reinstatement fee.

Purchasing Books and Supplies

Campus bookstores are notoriously expensive, so when you get your reading list you might want to check for alternative bookstores in the area. Large universities usually have independent bookstores on the fringes of the campus that specialize in used books and books at lower cost. You may also want to check to see if any of the online booksellers have the titles you need. Online bookstores often offer discounts, and some smaller online bookstores are specifically geared toward students. Check out www.amazon.com and www.barnesandnoble.com, which are two of the largest online booksellers. In addition to potential savings, your books will be delivered to your home and may save you from waiting in long lines at the campus bookstore.

SURVIVAL STRATEGIES

- Check the bookstore for required texts for each course. Compare cost and availability of books with alternative bookstores nearby or by checking out online bookstores.
- It is a good idea to purchase textbooks early, as many university bookstores order fewer books than are actually required for the total number of students in the class.
- Consider sharing the costs of expensive textbooks with a classmate.
- See if any required or optional textbooks are available to be checked out at your university library (you will have to move early to take advantage of this alternative, since other students will likely be doing the same thing).

Becoming Familiar with the School and University/College Services

School services can help you cope with stress. Most colleges and universities have adequate resources for almost every need. These include learning resource centers, computer laboratories, a library, a counseling center, a health center, disabled student services, a career planning center, athletic facilities, and a variety of university-wide interest groups. The school of social work probably also has helpful resources such as an on-site social work library, a social work student organization, and a social work computer lab. Available services will be listed in the university catalog and social work bulletin.

SURVIVAL STRATEGIES

- Read through the university catalog and social work bulletin, and list all the resources you think you will need.
- Visit the location of these resources before you actually have a need to use them.
- Find out how the health center operates and the operational hours of the library, computer labs, pool, or workout rooms. This will save you time and frustration.

Becoming Familiar with the School and University/ College Procedures, Regulations, and Protocols

Every university has certain procedures, regulations, and protocols, which they expect students to observe and follow. This is usually true of each school of social work as well. Neglecting careful attention to the rules and regulations has resulted in more than one student's dismissal from a social work program. For instance, some universities forbid alcohol or illicit substances on campus, including in residence halls. Use of substances on campus or driving under the influence on campus may result in dismissal from the university. Most programs also have explicit rules and consequences about plagiarism, cheating, and timely submission of assignments. Rules, procedures, and regulations are generally clearly specified in the university and program documents. Unfortunately, students often fail to read these documents carefully.

SURVIVAL STRATEGIES

- Carefully read the university catalog and social work program bulletin, and fully familiarize yourself with what will be expected of you.

- Carefully read each course syllabus and outline for specific expectations and guidelines.
- If you are not certain you understand what plagiarism is, go to the university writing center and ask for a session specifically designed to help you understand.

If your instructors require that you adhere to the American Psychological Association (APA) writing style for paper and manuscript preparation, make certain that you have a copy of the latest version (usually found in the university bookstore). Read the manual and learn how to use the writing style *before* you begin working on your assignments. If you are uncertain as to its correct use, consult the university writing center or your instructor for assistance.

Most graduate programs today also require extensive use of the computer. This may entail word processing, use of the Internet, spreadsheets, and data analysis. If you are not computer literate, it is critical that you become so before entering graduate school. Trying to keep up with the work demands of graduate school while also learning to master the computer is virtually impossible. Find out from your graduate school the level of computer literacy expected of students and the hardware and software available in the computer labs in the school of social work, library, and across the university. It will be most useful to have computer and software compatible with the computer lab at the social work program. Become proficient in the programs before you start classes.

Most graduate social work programs are quite serious about the consequences associated with cheating. In addition to some of the older forms of cheating we are all familiar with, cheating also includes taking papers off the Internet and submitting them as your own and using a paper you wrote for one class and submitting it for another without the instructor's prior consent. Turning assignments in on time is also taken very seriously in graduate school. Consult your course syllabus and outline for due dates. Mark these dates on your calendar, and give yourself sufficient time to prepare and submit your assignments in a timely fashion. At the very least, most graduate instructors will deduct points for an assignment received late, and some instructors will not accept a late assignment at all.

Becoming Familiar with Student Organizations

Most schools of social work have three organizations available to students. These include a student social work association, a social work honor society, and a student membership in the National Association of Social Workers. Some schools of social work also have a student chapter of the National Association of Black Social Workers. Student membership in other related organizations may also be available. The availability of organizations to students is generally listed on the Web site of the school of social work, in the university bulletin, and in the social work program's bulletin. Membership and participation in these organizations can be an important source of learning associated with the profession and can provide peer support, guidance, and important networking opportunities for you with community agencies and experienced social work professionals.

SURVIVAL STRATEGIES

- Consult your university catalog and school bulletin to find out what student organizations are available to you.
- Talk with your faculty advisor and other students about membership in student and professional organizations. Find out when they meet and how you can become a member.

Membership for students in professional organizations is generally set at a very low fee. Although it is very important that you balance your school work obligations with outside interests, we strongly suggest that you become involved in your social work student organization and in at least one professional organization. The friendships and relationships you forge with other students will last throughout your professional career. These relationships will be beneficial well into the future for professional networking and career opportunities.

Equally important are the networking opportunities you will have as a student member in a professional organization. Experienced social workers often provide mentoring to students and young professionals and can be very helpful to you during your job search upon graduation. Working on committees in the student organization and/or in your professional organization can provide you with valuable work experiences, which are impressive on a resume and can demonstrate some of your organizational and administrative skills.

In this chapter, we have stressed the importance of preparing for entrance into the university and school of social work as much as possible *before* you arrive on campus to register and begin classes. Familiarity with policies, procedure, and protocols will help prevent anxiety, confusion, and mistakes and will help you feel more confident and comfortable. You will also convey to your faculty, advisors, and peers your commitment to your graduate education. So, learn as much as you can beforehand and don't be afraid to ask questions when you arrive on campus.

Chapter 5

UNDERSTANDING THE SOCIAL WORK CURRICULUM AND INTERNSHIP

At last you are enrolled and ready to begin your program of study. It is likely that you had relatively little choice in which courses to take, apart perhaps from choosing among different sections of the same class offered at different times with different professors. In fact, you may be disappointed in the apparent lack of opportunity for you to take interesting elective courses right away, either within your school of social work or in other departments at your university.

THE MSW CURRICULUM

Why isn't there more flexibility in your program of study? The reason is that in an effort to ensure some degree of standardization in the MSW curriculum, the Council on Social Work Education has some fairly strict guidelines about the types of courses to be offered in order for an MSW degree program of study to be accreditable. Although frustrating, it is understandable that the profession wishes to ensure some degree of comparability between the MSW awarded at your university and those offered by other universities. Surely you can understand the need for law students to receive a comparable curriculum across accredited law schools in the United States, or for medical students to cover the same topics in different medical colleges. For similar reasons, your own MSW program is fairly well structured.

The document that provides overall guidance on the structure of MSW programs is called the *Educational Policy and Accreditation Standards* (called EPAS from here on) and is produced by the Council on Social Work Education. You can get a copy by going to the CSWE Web site www.cswe.org and clicking on the Accreditation button. The EPAS will appear and can be printed out. Here is part of the preamble:

The Council on Social Work Education (CSWE) Educational Policy and Accreditation Standards (EPAS) promotes academic excellence in baccalaureate and master's social work education. The EPAS specifies the curricular content and educational context to prepare students for professional social work practice. The EPAS sets forth basic requirements for these purposes. (CSWE, 2001, p. 3)

Thus, all accredited MSW programs must abide by the common curriculum and policy standards found in the EPAS.

For those students completing a two-year program of study and who hold an undergraduate degree in a discipline other than social work, the first two semesters (or three quarters) are usually called the foundation year, and the second two semesters (or three quarters) are known as the concentration year. Most schools of social work do not require their students to attend classes or an internship during the summer. Some, however, may offer elective coursework that many students take for additional preparation or to reduce their course load the second year of the program. Or students may fulfill certificate program requirements above and beyond those needed to earn the MSW by going to school during the summer between the foundation and concentration years or during the summer following the concentration year. Students completing their degrees on a part-time basis may not follow this same regimented calendar, but their coursework and internship requirements are similarly denoted as foundation and concentration. Although they take longer to complete, the sequencing (i.e., linear ordering) of coursework and practice in part-time programs is usually similar to that required in the full-time program. According to the EPAS (CSWE, 2001, p.11) you must be taught the following content during your foundation year: values and ethics; understanding, affirmation, and respect for people from diverse backgrounds; populations-at-risk; the reciprocal relationships between human behavior and social environments; the history of social work, social welfare services, and the role of policy; knowledge and skills to work with individuals, families, groups, organizations, and communities; qualitative and quantitative research content; and field education.

Usually, but not always, schools of social work construct their curriculum by having a single course deal with each of the above issues, in effect compartmentalizing each topic. Hence, during your foundation year, you will likely have courses titled like those listed below.

Cultural Diversity

This course covers topics such as the similarities and differences among people of different racial, ethnic, and religious groups, as well as other aspects of diversity (e.g., sexual orientation, disability, etc.).

Social Welfare Policy and Services

This course covers the history and philosophies underlying contemporary welfare policies and services. Content on the critical analysis of welfare policy is also included, involving how policies affect various oppressed and marginalized groups of people.

Social Work Research

This course covers the basics of a scientific and analytic approach to knowledge building, including qualitative and quantitative research methods. Generally a strong component on the design and conduct of outcome studies of social work services research is included, stressing the use of group- and single-system research designs.

Social Work Practice with Individuals and Small Groups

This course provides a generalist perspective on micropractice (helping individuals, couples, families, and small groups). Collecting and evaluating data, interviewing skills, assessment, intervention, and termination issues are covered.

Social Work Practice with Communities and Organizations

This is the macropractice (helping communities, large groups, organizations, the larger society) equivalent of the individual practice course.

Human Behavior in the Social Environment

This course covers theories of human behavior and development, as well as understanding behavior across a range of systems (individuals, groups, families, organizations, etc.).

Foundation Practicum (also known as field instruction or internship)

This class involves agency-based, supervised, educationally focused work experience. A concurrent field seminar may or may not accompany this class.

Electives

Most programs allow for a limited number of elective courses.

During the concentration year, the required courses cover roughly the same content areas but are presumably more advanced or specialized. For example, the foundation research course usually surveys a large number of research approaches (observational, correlational, surveys, quasi-experimental and experiments, single-system designs, etc.) and teaches for *comprehension*, whereas the concentration-year research course is more focused on *learning to do* evaluation research. And elective offerings can be somewhat broader. Given the scope of the content required by the CSWE, you may now understand why there is so little flexibility in most MSW programs.

So while you might be chaffing at the apparent restrictions imposed on you, at least you will have an understanding of the reasons for these restrictions. Some programs try to infuse required content throughout the curriculum, as opposed to having it compartmentalized in an individual class. For example, one model infuses content on cultural diversity throughout all other classes (practice, research, policy, etc.), and such programs may not elect to offer this in a separate class. Or evaluation research content may be built into practice classes during the concentration year in lieu of a separate course in evaluation research. But typically, faculty structure the MSW program so that the content areas mandated by the CSWE are covered in specific courses. However, some programs do both—have a specific course on a given required topic (e.g., cultural diversity) and also ensure that this topic is addressed in a number of other classes that students take (e.g., a practice class also includes content on cultural diversity).

Hopefully during your initial MSW student orientation session you will be provided with an internally produced MSW student manual that details your required program of study and a checklist of what courses you are supposed to take each term. This type of checklist is called a program of study form. Thus, when it comes time to register, you can check to see what is offered, then match this against your program of study, and enroll in what you are supposed to take.

If your program permits you to take elective courses outside the SSW, by no means overlook this option. Carefully review the university's course schedule for the future semester, paying particular attention to graduate courses in psychology, sociology, education, and child and family development. You may well find a specialized class of great interest to you but perhaps not offered or otherwise available to you in the school of social work. Some of these courses may only be open to graduate students in particular programs (e.g., clinical psychology), and some may be open only with permission of the instructor, but others will be free for you to enroll in (it is a good idea to check with your MSW program academic advisor first).

If you really want to explore elective courses, consider enrolling during the optional summer term. Or, take advantage of tuition policies available at some universities that say that once you have enrolled for a certain number of hours of credit (say twelve or fifteen semester hours) equaling full-time enrollment, it does not cost you any more money to take another class. This is called "taking an overload." You may have to get special permission from your advisor to do this, and it may make your semester especially grueling, but if it is the only way you can take a much-desired class, give this option serious consideration. Another way to squeeze in extra courses is to see if you can take, apart from the regular MSW curriculum, courses in social work or another department that my be offered in the evenings or on the weekends. These courses may not be a part of your regular program of study, but if space is available, your advisor says it is okay, and you are willing to shoulder the extra workload, this option is worth consideration.

FIELD EDUCATION

For many students, field education (also known as the practicum or internship) is perhaps the most exciting aspect of earning the MSW. Here is what the EPAS (CSWE, 2003, p. 10–11) has to say about field education:

Field education is an integral component of social work education anchored in the mission, goals, and educational level of the program. It occurs in settings that reinforce students' identification with the purposes, values, and ethics of the profession; fosters the integration of empirical and practice-based knowledge; and promotes the development of professional competence. Field education is systematically designed, supervised, coordinated, and evaluated on the basis of criteria by which the students demonstrate the achievement of program objectives ... field education ... provides for a minimum of ... 900 hours for masters students. (p. 10–11)

How all of the above gets played out in practice varies immensely across schools of social work, but a common model is something like the following: The SSW has a particular faculty member designated as director of field practicum (or some similar title). He or she is responsible for approving agencies to be used as practicum sites; recruiting and approving field instructors: those agency staff (usually social workers) who will be providing you with on-site supervision; helping to match both first- and second-year MSW students with placements, which (hopefully) support their personal interests and professional career objectives; working with the faculty to monitor your progress during each term of practicum; and intervening if things go wrong, advocating on your behalf within the agency if necessary, or perhaps even finding you a new placement.

The practicum director usually works with the other MSW faculty in the following manner. Most faculty are assigned certain practicum agencies to be responsible for, and these faculty serve as the school's most direct link between the MSW program and the agency. Want to learn more about a particular agency? Find the name of the faculty member assigned to coordinate with that agency and go see him or her. When fulfilling this linking role between agency and SSW, the faculty member is called a faculty liaison.

Sometimes students in practicum have a weekly or biweekly meeting called an integrative seminar. These meetings last for a couple of hours and are conducted by a faculty member and a number (say two to twelve, sometimes more) of MSW students. This integrative seminar may be offered for separate semester hour course credit, or its time may be built into the practicum course load. Its purpose is to provide the students in the field with support and an information network of peers who discuss and learn from their common experiences, hopes and fears, failures and successes. In the integrative seminar, sometimes there are readings you work through and sometimes it is less structured. Integrative seminars may be offered during block placements (when students are in placement only) to provide an academic anchor for MSW interns working in disparate agencies, during concurrent placements (when students are in classes and placements) only, or during both types of practicum arrangements.

Most schools do not want you contacting agencies about placement possibilities on your own. Always make such contacts only after getting approval from that agency's faculty liaison or your practicum director.

Another information mechanism that some schools of social work and practica offices support is to have an up-to-date ring binder describing the various available potential practicum agencies; this may also be accessible on your school's Web site. See if your school has something like this binder available.

Many schools ask you to fill out a practicum application for your foundation practicum. Sometimes this must be submitted even before you begin classes. Based on a number of factors, such as the practice interests expressed on your practicum application, your resume, past work experience in the human services, and your personal statement submitted when you applied to the MSW program, the practicum director will either assign you to a particular agency for your foundation practicum or direct you to a particular agency's faculty liaison for an appointment to discuss the possibility of placing you at that agency. The next stage in the process is likely a placement interview conducted at the agency, usually with that agency's field instructor(s). This interview is important. You should approach it as you would a job interview. Use your manners when you call and make the appointment; state that you have been referred to the agency by a professor in your school of social work, as a potential practicum student, and that you would like to schedule a meeting with the field instructor at his or her convenience (hopefully the faculty liaison has already ascertained that the agency is indeed interested in having one or more students in the upcoming academic term). Show up for this appointment on time, dressed in your business attire, and looking rested and well-groomed.

Bring a couple copies of your resume and a list of prepared questions you may wish to ask the field instructor. A sample of potentially relevant questions you may wish to ask is listed in box 5.1.

Use common sense during your interview. Although it is true that you are judging how well the agency and field instructor will meet *your* learning needs, the process is actually more of a "sell" of you to them, rather than the other way around. Do not approach the process as a skeptical know-it-all. Keep in mind that most agencies and field instructors serve as a host and supervisor to MSW students out of the goodness of their hearts, and it likely costs them far more in time, training, and office resources to provide this important aspect of your MSW training than they receive back in services to their clients.

On the other hand, practicum is crucial, and you are the "consumer," paying lots of money in tuition and devoting lots of time to the practicum setting, so some mild questioning is certainly appropriate on your part.

A judicious balance of assertiveness and acquiescence is called for. Accept the fact that you will likely have little choice in the foundation placement process, but be assertive in making your learning needs known with respect to the concentration (e.g., second year) practicum. If you clearly stated your desire on the second-year practicum application to gain assessment and intervention skills in the field of substance abuse counseling, have taken course electives in that area, written term papers on the topic, and are planning a master's thesis or research project on it, then finding yourself assigned to a placement unrelated to substance abuse may be a jarring experience. Work with your academic advisor in an effort to have him or her advocate on your behalf with the practicum director for an internship setting more congruent with your long-term career goals. It is not a good idea to deliberately attempt to sabotage your placement interview in the hopes that you will end up with your first-choice placement. Rather portray yourself in the best light. If the agency accepts you as an MSW intern, but you really do not want to go there, simply let the practicum director know and request to interview at alternative sites.

BOX 5.1   Potential Questions to Ask Field Instructors When Interviewing for a Potential Practicum Placement.

• Have you supervised students from our school of social work before?
• How frequently will I meet with you for supervision?
• How is supervision provided? One-on-one, or in small groups?
• Does the agency have an overarching theoretical orientation or practice model it embraces?
• What are your agency's major approaches to assessment? To intervention?
• Are the social work services provided at this agency supported by the empirical practice-research literature? To what extent?
• What type of orientation experiences do you provide for incoming interns?
• Have you ever hired any of your practicum students once they have graduated with the MSW?
• Do you have an MSW? Are you licensed to practice social work in this state? Surprisingly, many schools of social work use individuals who are not MSWs as field instructors. This is particularly common during foundation placements. We suggest that you try to obtain a placement, foundation or concentration, with an appropriately licensed MSW field instructor.
• Do you have any other advanced practice credentials?
• What types of practice experiences would I be provided?
• Will I need to use my own vehicle for my work in this agency? If so, am I reimbursed for my work-related mileage? How much?
• Are MSW interns provided a stipend or other benefits? (Surprisingly, most MSW practica do not pay interns. Be prepared for this.)
• Does the agency provide any in-service training for its staff that I can attend?
• Do you have any examples of learning contracts you used with previous MSW interns that I may look at?
• Have any of your previous MSW interns failed practicum, or have any been removed from this placement? Why?
• How many hours a week am I expected to work? What are the days? Is there any flexibility in scheduling these hours?
• Do you require MSW interns to work any evening or weekend hours?
• What are the clients like? For what particular problems or issues do they seek help?
• Have any MSW interns or staff ever been physically injured while working here? If so, what were the circumstances?
• Have there ever been any instances of sexual harassment or discriminatory treatment of MSW interns at this agency?
• Can you give me the names and phone numbers of any recent MSW interns who you supervised?

These questions are in no particular order and may not be relevant to all agencies. Some personal judgment is required to determine their applicability to the placement being considered.

Safety issues are a real and legitimate concern of students completing their practicum. If your proposed placement presents unacceptable real or potential risks to you and you have reasonable grounds to fear for your safety—fears of such magnitude that you are unwilling to accept such a placement—*do not* hesitate to say so and to request an alternative practicum assignment. Although he or she may not like the extra work late in this time-intensive process, it is the job of the practicum director to arrange student/agency matches that are satisfactory to both parties. If you try to arrange an alternative internship late in the process, compromises on your part may well be necessary. Desired placements may be filled already or simply unavailable. Agencies used in the past may no longer accept interns. Talented field instructors may retire, take a new position, or die, causing a long-term placement program to collapse. A particular agency you have your heart set on may not be an approved practicum training site.

Questions about sexual harassment, intern injuries, or unreimbursed expenses can be difficult to ask (particularly by relatively powerless MSW students), but know that these are very real and legitimate issues (see Tully, Kropf, & Price, 1993). MSW interns are sometimes sexually harassed, can be asked to use their own car in practicum without reimbursement, or are sometimes injured on the job. We are not saying that difficult placements should be avoided by MSW interns. Indeed, working in particularly challenging areas can be very rewarding. But we do suggest that you go into such situations with your eyes wide open and with a realistic appraisal of the risks and benefits involved. And the only way you can do so is by respectfully asking about such issues.

You should approach the placement process in a spirit of cooperation and good will. Ideally it will work out to be a terrific learning experience for you, even if you initially have some doubts. But do not passively accept a placement in an agency that has a history of abusing interns, of interns being assaulted by clients, or of failing to provide satisfactory supervision. If you have qualms, discuss them with your faculty advisor. If unresolved, you should then go to the practicum director. If an untenable situation persists, the MSW program director for your SSW, followed by the associate dean, then dean are the appropriate channels to follow, in that order. Do not directly call the university president (or even the social work dean or director) and angrily demand that they intervene to resolve your problems. Follow the chain of command. If you go directly to the president or dean, a good administrator will ask you if you have tried to resolve the matter using your academic advisor or the practicum director. If not, you will likely be gently ushered out the door and urged to work with those people first.

Very rarely, you can set the wheels in motion to get a new practicum site approved for MSW-student placements. Generally, such student-initiated efforts are frowned on by faculty, who feel that they have sufficient, satisfactory placements available. But, if a really great potential placement exists, you can gently inquire with the practicum director how it could get approved so that you could possibly be placed there. If he or she is mildly receptive, offer what help you can to expedite the process. If you are successful, you may not have arranged a great learning experience only for you, but also for other MSW interns in the future.

The EPAS require that the nine hundred clock hours (that is a minimum; many schools require more) of practicum be divided between the foundation and concentration years. (Advanced standing students are required to have four hundred hours of field education.) A common practice is to have about four hundred hours in the first year and five hundred or so during the second year in a different agency. The rationale for using different agencies it to provide you with exposure to an array of social services, more services than you would obtain at a two-year placement in the same setting. This variety is a good idea but frustrating to the first-year student who winds up in a placement with an ideal field instructor, a supportive faculty liaison, and in a hospitable agency. Another reason is that the level of complexity in the services provided may mitigate against using the same placement for both foundation and concentration years. Hopefully, your concentration practicum will provide training in more sophisticated assessment and intervention skills than those obtained in the first year's placement.

Although schools of social work do have some degree of latitude in how they structure their practica, the actual choices are relatively few. One factor is whether schools institute concurrent or block placements. In the concurrent model, you attend classroom-based classes and at the same time spend two to three days per week in an agency-based practicum. In the block model, you attend only classroom instruction one semester, and only practicum for four to five days per week another semester. Some schools of social work use concurrent practica during both the foundation and concentration years, others use block placements during both years, and still others alternate, with block (or concurrent) the first year, and concurrent (or block) the second year. A further permutation is that some schools permit or require enrollment in practica during the summer, and yet another wrinkle is the variations followed in part-time MSW programs, as opposed to the more usual full-time programs.

Your MSW student handbook should clearly outline all this information for you, and the program of study form should indicate how many semester and clock hours of practica are required each semester at your school of social work. Generally, advanced standing students (those who previously earned a CSWE-accredited BSW degree) are exempt from all foundation practica and enroll in graduate social work courses for the first time in the summer term and then take didactic classes and a concurrent practicum during the subsequent fall and winter terms, or didactic classes during the summer and fall, followed by block practicum during the winter.

Specialized concentrations (e.g., school social work) or certificate programs (e.g., gerontology, marital and family therapy, behavior therapy) may pose additional requirements pertaining to the nature of your curriculum and practicum settings. For example, the need for school social workers, determined by the academic calendar of the public school setting, may not mesh well with the academic calendar of the university and school of social work practicum schedule, so special arrangements are developed by the director of practicum and the coordinator of the certificate program. Obviously, someone completing a certificate in gerontology or behavior therapy would be placed in a concentration practicum providing explicit training in those areas.

Problems in Practicum

Most students have a productive and relatively problem-free learning experience during their foundation and concentration practica. But we would be disingenuous to pretend that problems do not arise. Sometimes these problems are external to the student; a field supervisor may leave the agency or a program may lose its funding. Other times problems are due to actions (or inactions) on the part of the MSW intern. Whatever the reason, do not panic. Your school is committed to working these problems out with you, resolving them in your present practicum site, or arranging a new placement. The exceptions to this are obvious—financial wrongdoing on your part, serious ethics violations, sexual harassment or inappropriate contacts with clients, and really egregious offenses that you have committed. In such cases, you had best quietly withdraw from the MSW program and seek a career in another field.

The major players in resolving problems have been mentioned before—you, your field instructor, your faculty liaison, the practicum director, your faculty academic advisor, the MSW program director, the associate dean, and the dean director of your school, in roughly that order. Documenting issues and/or problems is always a good idea. If you are receiving minimal supervision from your field instructor, and this is a problem, keep a record of broken appointments to support your concerns when you discuss it with him or her. If you are being asked to work too much, way beyond the usual number of clock hours, and without a compensatory time-off arrangement, keeping a log of your hours is helpful. Make sure your agency records and files are in order at all times, and do not sign off on things you are not fully prepared to take responsibility for.

Clinical issues can usually be resolved with the agency supervisor and faculty liaisons. If you were seriously abused as a child and you are inadvertently assigned to work with a client who bears a striking similarity to the person who harmed you twenty years ago and this is interfering with your ability to effectively work with this client, do not let the problem fester. Deal with it early on in your supervision, and do what is necessary to reassign the client or otherwise make it possible for you to help him or her.

If someone at the agency is sexually harassing you, confront the perpetrator early on and make your complaints clear, specific, and to the point. Tell the person that if it happens again you will file a complaint. If the episode was really awful, skip this step and file a complaint right after discussing it with your field instructor. If the field instructor is the perpetrator, bring the issue to your faculty liaison. In gray areas ("Was he hinting he would like to date me?"), give the other person the benefit of the doubt until the harassment becomes less ambiguous. The school of social work has some responsibility to ensure that you are not exposed to harassment, danger, or exploitation in practicum, so do not hesitate to take action when such issues occur. Early action is always advised. It is likely that your college or university has a formal written policy defining what constitutes sexual harassment and steps to be taken in the event of a complaint. It is wise to familiarize yourself with this policy.

Although your practicum supervisor may recommend your grade to the faculty liaison, most schools reserve the privilege of assigning the actual grades to the faculty liaison, a real member of the SSW faculty who is the instructor of record. If you believe that you were unfairly graded, schedule a meeting with the person who assigned you the grade and calmly ask for the reason why you were awarded a C, D, or F. The faculty liaison should be able to take out the learning contract between you and the agency/practicum supervisor and clearly delineate the deficiencies in your performance. You would then know what you would need to do next term to improve your performance.

If you *really* believe that you have been unfairly graded, you can ask the faculty liaison to recommend changing your grade. You will be immeasurably aided in this effort if you can (with your learning contract or other documentation) delineate how you more than fulfilled the expectancies for the term and prove that any deficiencies mentioned by the liaison were the result of miscommunication or error.

If neither of the above scenarios results in a grade change, most schools of social work have an internal grievance procedure. This procedure should be clearly spelled out in your MSW student handbook. The procedure may involve working with your faculty advisor and sending a written appeal to the MSW program director. He or she will convene a small group (two to three) of uninvolved faculty to serve as a grade appeal committee, to review the documentation you can provide for a change of grade, and who will also review the justification for the low grade awarded by the faculty liaison. The appeal committee will make a recommendation to the associate dean or dean, who will either support the change of grade or not. This process can take weeks or months.

If your internal grade appeal is not resolved in your favor and you are *really* sure you want to pursue this, the next level is to take the appeal outside of the school of social work to the graduate school at your university or other larger academic unit in which your school or department is housed.

The ability to appeal a low grade or other academic decision is clearly seen as a right of graduate students. You need not be shy about exercising this right, but be sure that you do so judiciously, and not frivolously. In order for rights to be maintained, they should not be abused.

Separate from grade appeals and academic matters, most colleges and universities have some office or official who is responsible for investigating complaints about unequal treatment because of one's race, gender, religion, sexual orientation, etc., such as an office of equal opportunity, and a separate mechanism for investigating allegations of sexual harassment. Information about these complaint mechanisms should be found in your MSW student handbook and/or posted conspicuously on a bulletin board in a public location in the school of social work. Such offices may also be used to help obtain resolution about problems encountered during one's practicum.

You have at least two other mechanisms to remedy very serious issues of being maltreated as an MSW intern in practicum. One is the Code of Ethics of the National Association of Social Workers (NASW, 1997). This document describes how social workers should and should not act and governs the professional conduct of all members of the NASW. The very act of joining the NASW places one under the regulation of the Code of Ethics. In the code you find numerous guidelines for professional behavior (e.g., "Social workers should treat colleagues with respect. . . . Social workers should avoid unwarranted criticism of colleagues in communications with clients or with other professionals" [Standard 2.01], as well as explicit prohibitions (e.g., "Social workers should not sexually harass supervisees, students, trainees, or colleagues. Sexual harassment includes sexual advances, sexual solicitation, requests for sexual favors, and other verbal or physical contact of a sexual nature" [Standard 2.08]). If a social worker who serves as your teacher (classroom instructor, faculty liaison, practicum supervisor, etc.) is a member of the NASW and violates the Code of Ethics, you may wish to file an ethics complaint with the state chapter of the NASW. Contact your local NASW chapter to find out the procedures for doing this.

A related mechanism may apply if the perpetrator is a licensed social worker. The state licensing board will have a similar mechanism designed to investigate complaints of unethical behavior on the part of licensees. Contact the state board to request information on filing a formal ethics complaint of a licensed social worker acting under the scope of his/her license (and providing supervision and teaching may well be covered under the license).

Both of these latter approaches are powerful ammunition, indeed, and should be used sparingly and with great circumspection, preferably after alternative avenues of remedy have been exhausted.

In good schools of social work, the curriculum you will follow will be clearly explained to you orally during your initial orientation sessions and in writing in the school of social work's bulletin and MSW student manual. The choices of courses to take may be few or even ambiguous. Your academic advisor will be readily available and should provide genuinely helpful advice. The practicum director will be on top of her job and be successful in placing you with a well-qualified agency that has employed an enthusiastic licensed social worker to provide you with excellent supervision as you gain practice experience in an area of genuine interest to you. Your faculty liaison will stay in close touch, visiting you and your supervisor at the agency a minimum of twice per semester. The net result of all this support is that you sail smoothly through the MSW program and graduate happy to recommend your school of social work to prospective applicants.

References

Council on Social Work Education. (2003). *Educational policy and accreditation standards.* Alexandria, VA: Author.

National Association of Social Workers. (1997). *Code of ethics.* Washington, DC: Author.

Tully, C. C., Kropf, K. P., & Price, J. L. (1993). Is the field a hard hat area: A study of violence in field placements. *Journal of Social Work Education, 29,* 191-199.

Selected Terms Pertaining to the
MSW Curriculum and Practicum

advanced standing—An abbreviated MSW program that graduates of a CSWE-accredited BSW program may qualify for. Not all MSW programs offer an advanced standing option.

block placements—Practica taken four to five days per week, without concurrent enrollment in classroom-based courses.

Code of Ethics—A document produced by the NASW containing the ethical guidelines to which all members of the NASW are expected to adhere.

concentration year—The second year program of study leading to the two-year MSW degree.

concurrent placements—Practica taken at the same time the MSW student is taking classroom-based courses. Usually taken two to three days per week.

Council on Social Work Education (CSWE)—The sole organization authorized by the Council on Higher Education to accredit MSW programs.

Educational Policy and Accreditation Standards (EPAS)—The guidelines authored by the Council on Social Work Education containing the required content mandated for accredited MSW programs.

dean or director—The chief academic officer of a school, college, or department of social work. Usually deans head independent schools or colleges, while directors head departments.

faculty liaison—The school of social work faculty member (ideally a licensed social worker) who is the link between a given social service agency in the community and the school of social work. You work with this person in arranging your placement.

field instruction director (or practicum director)—The school of social work faculty member (ideally a licensed social worker) who administers the practicum office. Sometimes one faculty member deals with foundation practica, and another with concentration practica.

field instructor (or practicum supervisor)—The agency staff person (ideally a licensed social worker) who provides you with on-site direction and supervision during practicum.

field practicum—The nine hundred plus mandated clock hours required by the CSWE of agency-based, supervised, educationally focused job experience, also called field instruction, practicum, and internship.

foundation year—The first year of study leading to the two-year MSW degree. This may be exempted by advanced standing students.

HBSE—A commonly encountered acronym that stands for human behavior in the social environment. Also a nickname for a required MSW course dealing with the topic of human behavior.

integrative seminar—A small group of MSW interns who are taught by a social work faculty member and meet to discuss issues that arise during their practica.

MSW program director—The social work faculty member administratively appointed to direct the MSW program. Usually answers to the dean or associate dean.

NASW—The National Association of Social Workers, the major (more than 160,000 members) professional social work organization in the United States.

Chapter 6

SCHOOL SERVICES

Most graduate schools of social work, as well as the colleges and universities in which they are housed, offer specialized services to students. Unfortunately, many students do not familiarize themselves with all that a campus has to offer. As a result, students may miss out on readily available services or information that can be enormously helpful to them during their graduate studies. Learning about all the resources available to you and how to access them ahead of time can save you time and effort in the long run.

THE STUDENT HANDBOOK

Almost every graduate school of social work has a student handbook. You should be provided with a copy of the student handbook when you are admitted to the graduate school or when you arrive at the school. You should become familiar with the student handbook. It will outline your rights and responsibilities as a student. A student handbook contains valuable information you will use throughout your tenure as a graduate student. You can expect that the student handbook will contain information about registration, academic and professional conduct, grades and grading, general requirements for graduation, proficiency examination, independent study, thesis or comprehensive examination, application for graduation, the student appeal process, withdrawal procedures, readmission procedures, access to student records, financial aid, student organizations, and information regarding field practice. The handbook is also a rich source of information on support services available to students.

YOUR ACADEMIC ADVISOR

Most schools of social work assign an academic advisor to each student when the student is admitted to the program. Your academic advisor will become an important person in your life as a graduate student. Your academic advisor can help you plan your course of studies from the beginning of the program through graduation. In most instances, you will see your academic advisor during each registration period. Some social work programs will not allow you to register for courses without approval from your advisor.

Academic advisors often provide graduate students with advice about the student's professional development as a social worker, in addition to academic counseling. They can help inform you about the profession, the range of practice possibilities, and the types of opportunities available to you for volunteer and field practice. The academic advisor often serves as a reference when the student graduates.

CAMPUS SAFETY

College and university campuses are as vulnerable to concerns of personal and property safety as any community is. College students are often viewed as easy prey by unscrupulous people because they tend to be so busy during their time on campus that they are not as observant of their surroundings as they could be. In recent years, crime has increased dramatically on some college campuses, and it is important that you familiarize yourself with security services available on campus.

All colleges and universities have security personnel on campus. You should obtain the phone number for the security office on campus and carry it with you in case of an emergency. Most campuses also provide services such as escort service at night, defense training, and safety training. All of these are important in preventing rape or assault on campus. We urge you to take advantage of all these services. Many campuses are not well lit at night. If you are taking night classes, it is a good idea to walk together in groups after class is over or to ask a friend or fellow student to walk you to your car.

Chances are that you will be taking all of your classes primarily in one or two buildings. You will get to know the personnel who work in these buildings and your fellow students well. This often creates a false sense of security for students. Thieves know this and know that students often keep their money and belongings in their backpacks, so it is important to keep them on your person at all times. Do not lay your personal belongings down in the library, student lounge, or hallway and walk away (even for a few minutes). This is especially important as the fall semester nears holiday break—a favorite time for thieves on campus.

Should you experience any crime on campus, report it immediately to the office of campus security.

STUDENT SERVICES

The Learning Resource Center

Most colleges and universities have a learning resource center. The services offered in the learning resource center differ from campus to campus. However, many offer specialized assistance in computer proficiency, report and essay writing, reading comprehension, and library research skills. These services are often offered on an individualized basis and can be very helpful to students struggling in a certain area. In most cases, individual appointments can be made for specialized assistance. It has been our experience that students with a specific weakness can correct the deficiency in a relatively short period of time through the help and support of trained experts available through the learning resource center. If a specific problem has been identified by one of your instructors, or if you know that you are not as strong in an area as you wish to be (such as writing), make an appointment at the learning resource center as soon as possible to begin to strengthen this area of weakness. It is critical that you not wait too long. Most graduate schools of social work require that each student maintain a relatively high grade point average (usually a minimum of 3.0) to remain in the program. A poor grade in one or two courses could result in your dismissal from the graduate program, if you do not improve your GPA after a term or two on academic probation. Taking care of deficiencies immediately can prevent disastrous consequences.

The Library

The college or university that you attend will have at least one library. Some schools of social work have their own social work library.

As a graduate social work student, you will spend quite a bit of time accessing and utilizing library materials. Most graduate social work programs offer an introduction to using the library as part of the new student orientation. Almost all libraries now offer reference services and intralibrary and interlibrary loan services. Reference services provide research assistance and access to commercially available databases. Self-searching of selected databases is usually available within the library and remotely, using the Web. Interlibrary and intralibrary services borrow monographs and obtain copies of other materials from libraries around the world, usually at minimal or no cost. However, there is usually some delay in receiving materials through the library loan service. This delay will require you to begin work on papers and projects early so that you can be assured that you will have all of the materials you will need in sufficient time. Today, most library holdings are accessible via sophisticated online catalogs, which can be searched from computer stations within the library or by remote computer access.

Student Counseling and Health Center

Almost all colleges and universities offer health services to any student who has paid a health fee. Some colleges include the health fee as part of an overall fee for full-time students. If you are a part-time student, you may have to pay an optional fee to receive the health services. Health services generally cover outpatient services delivered through a professional staff of primary care physicians, nurses, laboratory, and X-ray technicians. In addition, most university health clinics have a large network of referral sources for services that are not offered by the clinic. Student group health insurance is also offered through most colleges and universities. It is important for you to have hospitalization insurance because hospitalization is generally not covered through the health services fee.

The student counseling center, available on most college and university campuses, usually provides a variety of services for students with personal and academic concerns. The services help promote academic performance, increase personal growth, and contribute to the mental health of the university community. Services generally include crisis intervention, group therapy, individual therapy, academic counseling, outreach programs, and consulting help with program planning, adjustment, and personal problems.

Child Care

Not all colleges and universities offer child care services, but many do. The types of services and ages of children served vary across campuses. If you will need child care, a good place to begin searching for appropriate care is the university child care center. In addition to providing care, they generally offer an extensive referral service list.

Career Planning Center

Most universities and colleges have career planning and/or career placement centers. These centers provide career-related assistance to students through a range of programs and services. Usually included in these services are career or job fairs that provide students with an opportunity to speak informally with representatives from different companies about their entry-level jobs and hiring practices; nonprofit career fairs involving representatives from numerous area nonprofit organizations; employer information, which includes types of academic majors sought by the employer, job descriptions, career profiles, annual reports, and other pertinent information about various companies that recruit on the campus; and workshops providing instruction in skills and tactics for successful interviewing, resume preparation, business and dining etiquette, as well as other topics. Some centers administer a service allowing you to place your resume and letters of reference on file for prospective employers to review. Some centers also offer access to video conference interviewing, resume access via the Internet, and other state-of-the-art forms of placement assistance.

Women's Center

Not all colleges and universities have a women's center, but many do. On most campuses, the women's center provides essential information and referral services, a specialized collection of books and magazines about issues and concerns of women, and information on a variety of topics, usually including sex roles, violence against women, and spirituality. The women's center often offers educational, social, and cultural events pertaining to women's issues.

Disability Services

Virtually all universities and colleges have an office of disability services. The office of disability services seeks to work with disabled students to help them achieve and maintain individual autonomy and learn to eliminate any barriers they might encounter. The program's primary objective is to provide disabled students with access to on-campus academic, social, cultural, and recreational opportunities. Incoming students with a disability should contact disability services personnel so that they can be assured that the campus facilities and services are adequate to meet their needs. Contact with this office prior to registration enables the disability services staff to better assess the need for interpreters, readers, accessible facilities, and other support services. Van service is often provided to those individuals with mobility limitations. If you will require special accommodations in class or during examinations (such as extra time, access to a computer with software that magnifies words, a quiet space, a sign language interpreter, etc.), it is best to provide the office of disability services and your professor with ample time, well in advance of need. Some programs will not provide such special accommodations unless the student has registered with the office of disability services in advance. Documentation of disability from an attending physician or the student health center is usually required. The disability services office usually maintains strict confidentiality.

Minority Student Center

Many universities and colleges have a minority student center on campus. The purpose of most centers is to help retain minority students in school and to provide awareness and recognition of the accomplishments of minority Americans. Services provided generally include tutoring, group study sessions, workshops, a library collection of books and magazines, and social and cultural events.

Center for International Education

Most of the larger colleges and universities have a center for international education. These centers usually promote and support all aspects of international education and international exchange, both for American students and for students from other countries. For international students, the international center can provide information and assistance in matters relating to United States visa regulations, campus requirements for international students, campus academic policies and registration procedures, and insurance policies available to international students. International student advisors are generally provided along with a special orientation program for international students to promote adjustment to the campus and community. The center for international education may also provide advice about study-abroad options for American students, coordinate administration of international grants and scholarships for students, and provide information about other sources of funding for overseas study and research.

Campus Religious Organizations

Most colleges and universities, even public (and presumably secular) ones, have a large number of religious organizations affiliated either formally or informally with them. On or off campus you will likely find chapels, churches, temples, synagogues, or mosques dotting the landscape. Because they are aimed at relatively young people, these university-affiliated religious groups often hold regular social events, parties, day trips, social hours, singles nights, and more.

Becoming involved with a campus religious organization is a terrific way to ease your transition into an unfamiliar community.

SURVIVAL STRATEGIES

- Access the college or university Web site to ascertain all the resources available to you as a graduate student. Also access the graduate social work program's Web site for specific services and instructions available to you as a graduate social work student. Make note of all the services available. You may even wish to make a notebook of these services for easy reference. If Web sites are not available, peruse the university/college catalog for a listing and description of services. Services available for graduate social work students should be listed either in the social work program catalog, bulletin, or in the student handbook.

- Acquire a copy of the student handbook from the social work program to which you have been admitted. Some social work programs have a copy of the student handbook on their Web site. Others may provide you with a hard copy when you are admitted. Read through the handbook thoroughly before classes begin. Be certain that you are aware of all policies affecting you as a graduate student, your rights, and your responsibilities.

- Learn who your assigned academic advisor is. Find out the office hours of your advisor, and make an appointment to see him or her. Get to know your advisor well, and schedule regular appointments with your advisor each semester for academic and registration advice. Most academic advisors are extremely busy during peak registration periods. Be sure to make appointments to see your advisor early. Your academic advisor may also provide you with advising for the profession and may serve as a reference for you when you graduate.

- Ascertain the location of the university/college library and where the library holdings for the social work program are housed. Become familiar with the library and social work holdings early in your graduate studies, and preferably before you begin the program. If you are not skilled in using the library, database searches, or information Internet searches, make an appointment early to acquire these skills. These are skills that you will use often throughout your career as a graduate student. Students proficient in these skills can save themselves time and produce higher quality papers and projects.

- Find out if your university or college offers computer student access accounts to allow you to access the databases and conduct online searches from a remote station via modem (in other words, from your home computer). If available, apply for an account and learn how to use the systems as soon as possible. Being able to conduct library searches from home on your computer can save you time waiting for a computer station at the library and allow you to conduct your searches at times convenient for you.

- Find out if your university or college offers health and counseling services. Determine if there is an assessment of a health fee to cover these services and the extent of coverage of the services offered. Locate the health and counseling clinic so that you will be familiar with the location should you need these services.
- If you have a disability, contact the office of disability services prior to registration. Discuss your needs with disability services personnel, and make certain that the college or university can accommodate your needs. It is important that you give the office sufficient notice for them to arrange services to meet your needs in a timely manner. You should maintain frequent contact with the disability services office.
- If you will need child care while attending school, see if your university or college of choice has a child care center on campus. Find out if there are openings and what the cost of child care is. It is important to contact them early because university child care centers often have long waiting lists. They can also be helpful to you in locating baby-sitters or other forms of available local child care.

Learning what services are available through the university and social work program can be critical to your success in graduate school. As you can see from reading this chapter, most universities and colleges have an array of services to provide you with assistance and support. We encourage you to investigate all the services available and make use of those which are appropriate for you. Most faculty and staff at colleges and universities are there because they love working with students and are committed to helping you be successful, so don't be shy about looking into these resources.

Chapter 7

BECOMING LICENSED AND EARNING OTHER CREDENTIALS

As you approach the end of your MSW program, you will naturally become concerned about the standards pertaining to the legal regulation of social work in your state (or in the state to which you plan to move and practice). As in most things in life, accurate information is an essential element in your quest to become licensed. The process of obtaining accurate information is complicated because licensure or other forms of legal regulation of social work practice is the prerogative of the states. Your state—not the National Association of Social Workers, not the Council on Social Work Education, and not the federal government—determines the standards and qualifications for licensure. And, perversely, it seems like the states, the District of Columbia, Puerto Rico, and the Virgin Islands have covertly decided on a plan to make things as different as possible. So, the first step in your quest for accurate information consists of finding out what *your* state requires. Remember, licensure requirements vary widely from state to state.

The first thing you should do is locate the address and phone number of your state's governmental board that legally regulates the practice of social work. It will be called something like State Board of Social Work Examiners, or, in states that use a multidisciplinary board (as in Georgia), something like, The Composite Board of Professional Counselors, Social Workers, and Marriage and Family Therapists. You can find comprehensive listings of the addresses of these boards in a number of sources. For example, Ginsberg's (1998) book *Careers in Social Work* has an appendix that lists the names, addresses, and phone numbers of all the state boards, as does Barker's (2003) *Social Work Dictionary*. You can also try the NASW's Web page, www.naswdc.org, or the Web page of the Association of Social Work Boards (formerly the

American Association of State Social Work Boards [AASSWB]), at www.aswb.org. With a little hunting and searching on these Web pages, you will find your state board's address. (With the recent addition of a Canadian province as a member of the AASSWB, the group decided to trim its name to the more accurate ASWB.)

Next, call or write your state board (or that for the state to which you plan to move and go to work in) to ask for a licensure application package for new MSWs. In due course, this package will be sent to you and should contain a number of items, including a copy of your state laws and rules regulating social work.

This may be an impressive legal-looking document, full of headings and subparagraphs. Take the time to read these pages very carefully. It is boring but important. The laws are the heart of how you get licensed, and the accompanying rules describe how these laws are interpreted and put into action by your licensing board.

Before describing how to become licensed, we would like to review the importance of actually becoming licensed to practice social work. In many states, you will not be allowed to practice, or to use the title *social worker* (or related terms like *licensed clinical social worker, licensed independent social worker, registered social worker,* etc.) without a state license. You will likely be informed during your MSW program what your state's requirements are in this regard. Some states even require MSW student social work interns to be registered or licensed as social workers. So as a practical matter you need to prepare to get your license even before you obtain your first professional position after earning your MSW. Some states do allow newly minted MSWs the opportunity to work for several years under appropriate supervision prior to applying for one's license.

Another more noble reason to get your license is the added element of consumer safety that state licensure is supposed to promote. By ensuring that state-approved social workers have earned an accredited MSW degree, have some years of work experience, have passed a state or (more likely) national-level standardized examination that presumably attests that one is minimally qualified to practice safely, have passed a criminal background test (to exclude violent felons, sex offenders, or drug dealers from becoming licensed), the safety of the public receiving social work services is presumably enhanced.

Once you learn if licensure is required in the state where you intend to practice and have obtained a social work license application packet, you can set about completing this laborious but important process.

WHAT YOU WILL NEED

The Application Form

This form, which should be neatly typed or word processed, will ask you to provide names(s), addresses, phone numbers, any military service, and a series of yes-no questions (such as, "Have you had a license to practice a profession revoked, suspended, or otherwise sanctioned?" or "Have you been convicted of any felony or of any crime involving moral turpitude?"), and something about your other qualifications, such as having a CSWE-accredited MSW degree, names of references, etc. Fill out all these forms scrupulously and truthfully. You will be asked to explain any inconsistencies in the series of yes-no questions. Finally, you will be asked to attest to the truthfulness of your answers. Failure to provide accurate information can be grounds for revocation of licensure. Do not attempt to lie here.

Transcripts or Diploma

You may be asked to provide an official copy of your transcripts reflecting your graduation from a CSWE-accredited MSW program, and maybe also a copy of your MSW diploma. There may be a social work education verification form for you to send to your MSW program, asking them to fill it in, sign and seal it, and then return it to you (or sometimes to the state office). This would then accompany your application.

Letters of Reference

Nearly everyone will ask you to provide a few letters of reference from individuals familiar with your professional work. These are usually completed using a standard recommendation letter form sent with your application packet and may or may not need to be supported by a separate letter.

Supervision

Depending on your state's requirements, you must provide documentation of suitable supervised work experience. Again, if this documentation is required, the application packet will contain the supervision verification forms. Just make sure that the person you ask to verify your experience is qualified (as determined by the state) to provide you with supervision.

Application Fee

Do not forget to submit the required application fee (usually $100 or more) along with your application packet. Not enclosing the fee will mean a delay in the process and in your getting your license. Keep in mind that this fee is merely the application fee. You will also have to pay to take the written examination, and down the road, more still to renew your license and earn required continuing education hours, but more on that later.

The ASWB *Candidate Handbook*

Along with your state-provided materials, your application packet will contain a booklet prepared by the Association of Social Work Boards (ASWB) called the *Candidate Handbook*. This little document is packed with useful information about the test you will be taking and how to register to take it. There are four steps (the booklet walks you through them):

1. Make sure you are eligible to take the test. Your state licensing board will notify you when you have been approved to do so, *after* they have received everything else and it is in order. Once approved, if you will need special accommodations to take the test, contact your state board *before* registering for the exam so that suitable arrangements can be made for you.
2. Make sure you know which examination you will be taking. Again, the board will tell you about this, but double-check, because once you send in your money, there are no refunds.
3. Complete the examination registration form contained in the booklet (name, address, SSN, DOB, credit card information,

where you got your MSW, any special accommodations needed) and then *call* ASWB (the number is on the form) and register. You may also register by postal mail or fax if you prefer.

4. The ASWB will send you an authorization letter containing the exam category you may take, where your scores will be sent (most likely your state board), and how to set up an appointment at the testing site. Do this, and bring the letter with you to the testing site, along with a government issued photo ID (e.g., a driver's license or passport). You can take the test during normal business hours, Monday through Friday, and on Saturday in some locations.

We will have a lot more to say about the licensure examination later in this chapter. For now, read carefully the materials in your application packet about how to register to take the licensure test and take it at your convenience. Remember, the examination is usually taken after you have submitted all other materials for licensure. In most states you need state board approval to take the written examination, but a few do not require this approval. Check locally, and follow your state's requirements.

So, you have sent in your application packet (with accurate information, verification of education and supervision, and your fee), and you have been notified that you are eligible to take the written examination. Before discussing how to proceed, here is a little background.

WHAT IS LICENSURE AND WHY IS IT IMPORTANT?

This is an excellent question for you to ask, and although we can give you a general overview here in this chapter, we highly recommend two additional sources for more in-depth information. First, go to the library and see if they have a copy of *Professional Social Work Credentialing and Legal Regulation* (Thyer & Biggerstaff, 1989), which, although a bit dated, contains a good review of the history of the legal regulation of social work. It also contains a comprehensive annotated bibliography of articles and chapters dealing with licensure.

A second, more current resource is the Web page of the ASWB, mentioned above. The ASWB Web page contains truly comprehensive information about all aspects of licensure and the written examinations used in almost all states as a part of the licensure process. The ASWB was formed in 1979 and today consists of representatives from all states (and at least one Canadian province) that legally regulate the practice of social work. Its major function is to design, develop, validate, and administer the written exams used by the constituent states. But the ASWB does a lot more—it has developed a model licensure law that many states have adopted, it provides consultation and technical assistance to states in developing legal regulation, it approves and provides for continuing education for licensed social workers, it is a central resource for information on legal regulation of social work practice, and it is responsible for ensuring the accuracy and security of the test-taking process.

The authors have had some collaboration with the ASWB, and, in our opinion, it is one of the best-run organizations in professional social work today. These folks run a tight ship and do it competently and fairly.

The development of legal regulation of social work has been spurred by two concurrent developments: 1) the need to protect the public from incompetent practitioners and 2) the need for the social work field to acquire one of the essential characteristics of a true profession (in a sociological sense), a form of state-sanctioned, specialized expertise. Folks active in licensure will throw up their hands in dismay when they read the previous sentence, but in our opinion it is a truthful statement. There are decided and undeniable economic and professional interests advanced by the development of increasingly stringent laws covering the practice of social work, and it would be disingenuous to ignore them. However, we will focus on the consumer protection element of the arguments in favor of licensure and leave you to debate the less altruistic reasons for its existence among your classmates.

Licensure is an important element regulating the practice of many fields, such as medicine, law, and dentistry at one end, and mortuary science, cosmetology, and hairdressing at the other. You expect the person who repairs your plumbing to be licensed and to have presumably demonstrated a level of competence in her trade. As social work has grown to become the country's largest provider of mental health services, the need for increased legal regulation has become more compelling. To quote from the ASWB Web page:

> Regulation is designed to protect the public from unethical or substandard practice. A licensed social worker must meet minimum standards for education and experience, and usually must pass a licensing examination. Many states also require their licensed social workers to maintain and expand their competencies through continuing education. Every state in the country, as well as the District of Columbia and the U.S. Virgin Islands now use some form of social work regulation. For consumers, the regulation of social work provides two very important protections. First, legal regulation sets standards for competent practice— consumers know what to expect. Second, if those standards are not upheld, regulation gives consumers the power to lodge complaints that can result in sanctions or disciplinary actions against the social worker, or complete license revocation.

There are three related and sometimes confused terms covering the types of legal regulation.

1. A *registry* of social workers maintained by the state is a voluntary listing of social workers who are deemed competent to practice. But social workers are not required to be registered, and practitioners can call themselves social workers without being trained in that field.

2. *Certification* is a more stringent level of regulation, one which involves title protection—you cannot call yourself a social worker without being certified by the state.

3. Last, and most stringently, is actual *licensure*, which protects not only titles (e.g., without a license, you cannot call yourself a clinical social worker) but actual practices (e.g., psychotherapy, mental health counseling).

The trend is for states to go toward the direction of increasingly stringent standards, namely licensure involving the scope of practice. In this chapter, we will use the term *licensure*, assuming that you realize that this encompasses less restrictive forms of legal regulation such as registration and certification.

The states have evolved a complex multilevel system of licensure (unlike law or medicine). Although there are certainly specialties within these latter fields, there is only one level of licensure for medical doctors or lawyers. Not so in social work. Some states (only a few) license BSW-level social workers. The other three levels involve licensure for newly minted MSWs lacking any post-masters practice experience; licensure for those with two years of post-MSW supervised work experience; and licensure for those with two or more years of post-MSW, appropriately supervised *clinical* social work experience. A plethora of titles and acronyms are used to describe these varying levels of licensure, and a few of these are described in box 7.1. Do not let this bewildering array of titles and abbreviations confuse you. To some extent, this diversity reflects our relative immaturity as a profession. Over time,

BOX 7.1   Some Titles and Acronyms Used in Social Work Licensure

Acronym	Title
ASW	Associate Clinical Social Worker
BSW	Baccalaureate Social Worker
BCSW	Board Certified Social Worker
CAPSW	Certified Advanced Practice Social Worker
CBSW	Certified Bachelor Social Worker
CCSW	Certified Clinical Social Worker
CISW	Certified Independent Social Worker
CICSW	Certified Independent Clinical Social Worker
CMSW	Certified Master Social Worker
CSWM	Certified Social Work Manager
CSW	Certified Social Worker
LCSW	Licensed Certified Social Worker
LCSW	Licensed Clinical Social Worker*
LBSW	Licensed Bachelor Social Worker
LGSW	Licensed Graduate Social Worker
LISW	Licensed Independent Social Worker
LICSW	Licensed Independent Clinical Social Worker
LMSW	Licensed Master Social Worker
LSW	Licensed Social Worker
LSWA	Licensed Social Work Associate
PIP	Private Independent Practitioner
RSWA	Registered Social Work Assistant

*The most widely used designation for the independent clinical practitioner.

common sense within individual states (goaded perhaps by the ASWB and the NASW) will reduce the range of titles to just a couple.

The folks at the ASWB have prepared an array of written examinations for testing social workers at these varying levels of licensure. The four ASWB tests currently in place include the following: a *basic exam*, used by those states that license BSWs; an *intermediate exam*, used for newly graduated MSWs; an *advanced exam*, used for MSWs with two or more years of post-MSW practice experience; and a *clinical exam*, used for MSWs with two or more years of post-MSW practice experience in clinical social work.

The licensure application packet you receive from your state will tell you which level of test you will take, so be sure to apply to take the appropriate one (the intermediate examination will be the one encountered by most new MSWs).

All of the ASWB examinations consist of 170 multiple choice questions. One hundred and fifty of these are used to calculate your score, and twenty are experimental questions that may be used on a future test. Your responses to these twenty test items neither add to nor detract from your overall test score. These pretest items are randomly distributed among the test questions and (presumably) you will not be able to tell them apart from the real ones.

Each test item consists of an introductory statement or question (called the stem), one correct answer (called the key), and three incorrect answers (called the distractors). Every item is similarly formatted—there are no trick questions, no answers reading "all of the above," "none of the above," or a combination of responses, such as "A and B."

Potential test items are generated by social workers across the United States and by members of the ASWB Examination Committee. The test items are coded by content area and difficulty level and assigned to a particular level exam (basic, intermediate, advanced, clinical). Once the exam committee gives preliminary approval, the new item is put into a computerized database and is subject to being included as a pretest item on a future version of that test. After the item has been pretested on thousands of test takers its "performance" will be reviewed by the exam committee. Like Goldilock's porridge, a good test question is "just right"—not too hard and not too easy. An unsatisfactory question may be tweaked a bit by the exam committee (e.g., by amending a too tempting distractor) and replaced into the pool of pretest items, or it may be simply discarded. A satisfactory question is approved for use in future versions of a given level of exam.

Each version of a given level of exam is subtly different in terms of content but very carefully adjusted so that different iterations of the same test are virtually identical in terms of content areas covered and difficulty. In other words, the intermediate test you take today will be comparable in content and difficulty to the one taken by your friend six months ago, even though many of the questions themselves are different. This ensures comparability in test scores over time, and this process is conducted in the same manner as that done by the producers of the GRE and SAT tests.

Newly approved items are coded in terms of content area, which are related to core social work fields such as human development and behavior, diversity, assessment, micropractice, macropractice, interpersonal community, work-client relationship, values and ethics, supervision, practice evaluation and using research findings, and administration.

These areas vary a bit across the four levels of examination. For example, the clinical exam has much more on the diagnosis of mental disorders and on psychotherapy and clinical practice than does the basic exam.

Where do these content areas come from? To make a long story short, every decade or so the ASWB commissions researchers undertake a job analysis, wherein thousands of currently licensed social workers at all areas (BSW through advanced/clinical) of practice are surveyed about what they actually do on the job and what knowledge they make use of. The tests are then based largely on the results of these job analyses, with the clinical level exam based on the activities of real clinical social workers and the basic exam on those of BSW practitioners, etc. Although not a perfect way to develop content areas, it is difficult to come up with another way that is both fair and practical.

You will have up to four hours to complete the examination, which is now only available via computer, but at more than 250 test sites across the country. The test sites are owned by Sylvan Technologies, and there is likely one near you. If you have special needs (a visual or hearing impairment or learning disability), provisions will be made (in advance) to assist you. You are given plenty of time to familiarize yourself with answering multiple choice questions via the computer before beginning the actual test, and you may go freely back and forth among the items until your time is up. In other words, if you want to skip an item for later review you can do so. When you complete the test, you can then freely range back and forth over the questions and your answers, up to the four-hour time limit. The ASWB has worked very hard to make this way of taking the test as user-friendly as possible.

When you do take the ASWB test, your particular state may also require that you complete a separate examination on the laws regulating practice in that state. You will be sent information about registering for and taking this test as well.

You may really dread taking the ASWB exam at a visceral level, but some readers may have reservations about a competence certification program that makes use of standardized tests. Is this really the best way to determine who can practice clinical social work? Maybe not. We certainly recognize that the whole process has problems. For example, take the usefulness and validity of letters of recommendation, or the validity of quality-control issues centered around supervision. Whether or not you have reservations about parts of the licensing process, the whole process was established by the profession and for the time being this is the way it runs. If you don't like it, hold your nose, tip-toe your way through it, and get licensed (or engage in some form of social work that is not legally regulated). Once licensed you will have greater opportunity to work to improve the credentialing system.

HOW SHOULD I PREPARE TO TAKE THE LICENSURE TEST?

There are several schools of thought about preparation for taking the licensure examination. Namely, review the *Candidate Handbook* provided by the ASWB along with your licensure application materials. Look over the sample items and judge for yourself. If you are insecure about passing the test (remember, the majority, 70 percent, of first-time test takers pass it), then order the official study guide offered by the

ASWB, appropriate for the test you will be taking (most likely the intermediate or advanced exam). Information on ordering the correct study guide will be included in the ASWB booklet you were sent (you can also order them at the ASWB Web page or by calling 1-800-225-6880). The cost is a modest $25, plus $3 shipping. The study guides are about sixty pages long and contain everything you could ever want to know about the test, including the very best versions of fifty-item practice tests you can find. Correct answers are provided, and you can score yourself to see how you will do. For the new MSW graduate, this is pretty much all you will need to prepare to take the test.

Get plenty of sleep the night before and watch your caffeine intake. Other social workers may be taking the test in the room with you, or you may be the only one. In any event, you will have a private computer carrel. You can't bring anything in with you, like notes, books, or articles. You are on your own!

But What about Licensure Preparation Courses?

We do not recommend that you spend hundreds of dollars enrolling in either a home-based self-study program, Web-based tutorial, or a live-instruction preparation course in order to pass the social work written exam. Literally thousands of social workers take and pass these examinations every year without buying a commercial examination preparation program. You will learn that there are a number of individuals and firms around that advertise their test preparation program, and some even have ads in the *NASW News* and other professional outlets. We believe that these courses cater to the fears of anxious students and that most folks can take and pass the exam without excessive preparation. For example, the Web page for the firm Social Work Examination Services, Inc. has a small graphic on their title page with creepy looking writing on it that reads, **"Licensing Examination Anxiety? Fear No More with Comprehensive Study Guides from SWES!"** The flyer for the firm Social Work Licensure Examination Study Manuals states, "Don't lose precious time, energy or sleep worrying about the examination. Take the advantage: Order now and prepare to pass the examination!"

A few of the firms that have Web pages advertising their licensure preparation programs are listed in box 7.2.

BOX 7.2   Selected Social Work Examination Preparation Study Courses

---

Association for Advanced Training in the Behavioral Sciences
5126 Ralston Street
Ventura, CA 93003
(800) 472-1931
www.aatbs.com
   (They advertise a 97 percent pass rate.)

Berkeley Training Associates
1635 Solano Avenue
Berkeley, CA 95707
(800) 282-4122
www.btatraining.com
   (They advertise a 91 percent pass rate.)

Academic Review
30 East 60th Street, Suite 1007
New York, NY 10022
(800) 225-3444
www.areview.com
   (They advertise a 95 percent pass rate.)

Social Work Examination Services
132 Naples Road, South
Brookline, MA 02446
(800) 933-8802
www.swes.net

Social Work Licensure Examination Study Manuals
Ventajas, LLC
6547 Sperryville Pike
Boston, VA 22713
(877) 793-9267

Social Work Licensure Review
www.licensure.net

---

*These programs are not being recommended by the authors, but are merely listed here for interested readers.

You of course can check these out and make your own decision about whether or not to order them. A good, low-cost compromise is to find a licensed person who ordered a self-study exam prep course and ask to borrow their materials and practice tests (after all, they won't need them anymore, if the programs really do what they are supposed to).Your could even offer to pay them something for the materials. New materials and study programs may run up to several hundred dollars. What do you get for your money? Most home study programs provide:

1. written materials that supposedly address the substantive content (theory, DSM, practice, ethics, research, supervision, etc.), which appears on the actual examinations;
2. one or more sample tests that are supposedly comparable to the real thing;
3. oodles of sample questions supposedly like real items on the tests;
4. bibliographies (lists of readings)—that if you study on your own will supposedly help you do better on the actual test; and
5. tips on test-taking skills, how to relax, how to make the best guess as to the right answer, etc.

Much of this is all bundled into an impressive three-ring binder and used as a syllabus for a weekend course preparation workshop or as a home study course.

The last firm listed in box 7.2, www.licensure.net, does not offer a formal live-training program but rather Internet access to its comprehensive test bank (thousands of items supposedly like those on the real test) and test-taking tips, such as the following (this was taken from their Web page):

What do you do when you think you know the answer to a question but it is not a choice?
• Reread the question—maybe you didn't read the question correctly.
• Reread the question—maybe you didn't interpret the question the way they meant it to be interpreted.
• Reread the question—the test sometimes asks for the BEST of 4 choices and will have more than one correct answer.

You pay the fee (credit card over the Internet) to gain access to all the knowledge available on this site. Again, you be the judge as to whether or not this type of service (just look at the "tip" provided above!) would be useful to you. In most cases, our judgement is that it will not be.Take the practice test in the low-cost ASWB study guide, and if you do well, then sleep soundly and invest your hard-earned money elsewhere. If you want a home-based or Internet-based study course, share the costs with a few friends so that all of you can benefit.

The authors have significant reservations about the value of these home-study courses and Internet-based programs that are advertised as enhancing the likelihood you will pass the ASWB licensure examination. The cold hard facts are that very few people know in detail the questions that appear on each version of the examination. The testing company that is contracted by the ASWB holds all test items under conditions of the strictest security, and all the staff of the testing company and persons associated with the ASWB who come into contact with test items sign confidentiality agreements prohibiting their disclosing anything about these items. So, how do these exam prep firms come up with the "items" in their sample tests and battery of questions? Mostly, they query people who have recently completed the examination and ask them to reproduce items as best they can, from memory.

So here is the scenario—you have just completed a 170-item written ASWB licensure examination via computer. You are not allowed to make any notes to take away with you during the test itself. A person from an exam preparation study program contacts you (perhaps this was prearranged in return for payment—it happens!) a few days later and asks you to recall some of the items on the test. How many multiple-choice questions (with four possible answers) could you remember? How accurate could you be? These "recalled" items are then marketed by test preparation firms as representative of real items on the actual examinations. You can readily see how fraught with error such an approach is. The folks marketing these preparation programs actually have little idea about what is on the real tests. The problem for these firms is that the tests are constantly changing a bit with each administration. This makes it rather silly for you to pay hard-earned money to these "experts" for something in which they have very little expertise.

HOW IS THE ASWB TEST SCORED?

Your score is based on how many of the "real" items (150 out of 170) that you answer correctly. Your actual score will fall between 1 and 100, and this number does not correspond exactly with the number or percentage correct. Aggravatingly, each state sets its own passing score, so you cannot assume that a score of 70 is a passing score in your state, simply because a score of 70 is a pass in an adjacent state. Fortunately, you will be told your score before you leave the testing center. It will take three to four weeks for your state board to get your test results. If you scored sufficiently high enough, and everything else was in order, your license should arrive shortly.

What If I Fail?

If you do not get a passing score, plan to retake the test again soon (but ASWB policy is no sooner than ninety days). You will have to pay another testing fee. Some states limit the number of times you may retake the test. Check to see what your state's policy is.

WHAT ABOUT ALL THOSE OTHER CREDENTIALS?

Apart from the license to practice social work in your state, you may have encountered other forms of certification or credentialing and have some questions about their value and whether or not you should consider earning one or more of them. The short answer is no. As a soon-to-graduate MSW, focus on obtaining a job that will provide you with the type of appropriate practice experience necessary for you to qualify for, in a couple of years, the highest form of licensure offered by your state. Try to obtain a social work job wherein you will be provided suitable, documented supervision by a LCSW or other qualified supervisor who can sign off on your supervision verification form when you apply for licensure. Any credential or certificate for which you could qualify fairly soon after graduation is probably not worth the paper it is printed on. However, once you obtain the work experience necessary for advanced or clinical licensure in your state, then you may wish to reconsider some of these other credentials.

The National Association of Social Workers offers four certifications, and we will review each of these briefly before discussing credentials offered by other groups.

The Academy of Certified Social Workers

The ACSW was established in 1960 by the NASW to provide for certification of competence for self-regulated practice by individual social workers. It is a generalist credential only; it is not specifically a clinical social work certification. To apply for the ACSW you must:

1. hold regular membership in the NASW;
2. hold a CSWE-accredited MSW degree;
3. have at least two years of full-time, paid, supervised post-MSW work experience;
4. provide two suitable letters of recommendation;
5. complete the written application and send it in, along with the application fee;
6. complete and pass the ACSW written examination (a 150-item multiple-choice test).

In our opinion, the ACSW served a very valuable role in an era when few states provided for licensure or other regulation of the independent practice of social work. In fact, one of us (Bruce) maintained his ACSW for twenty years. However, with the rise of comparatively strict licensure laws, the relevance of the ACSW became less evident, and he recently dropped his membership. We recommend that you apply for membership in the ACSW if 1) you are in a job or are applying for a job that specifically requires you to have this certification; 2) if becoming a member of the ACSW provides some sort of employment benefit (e.g., a raise or promotion); or 3) if you simply want to support this practice credential offered by the NASW. You can learn more about the ACSW by visiting the NASW Web site www.naswdc.org and clicking on "credentials."

The School Social Work Specialist Credential

The school social work specialist (SSWS) credential was established in 1992 by the NASW to credential providers of social services and mental health services in school settings, including public schools, private schools, preschools, special education, and residential schools. Although some school systems require that their school social workers possess the SSWS credential, others simply prefer it, and most do neither. If you are, or wish to be, a school social worker, then this may be worth pursuing (in addition to the highest level of state licensure). Among the requirements for this credential are (1) a CSWE-accredited

MSW; (2) two years of documented post-MSW school social work employment and supervision; (3) references from a supervisor and a school social worker; (4) successful completion of the School Social Worker Specialty Area test (120 multiple-choice items); and (5) agree to follow the NASW Code of Ethics, the NASW's standards for school social work services, and the NASW adjudication process and also agree to obtain thirty verified clock hours of continuing education every three years.

Information on the SSWS credential can also be obtained on the NASW Web site.

The Qualified Clinical Social Worker

The QCSW credential is for those social workers who have met national standards of knowledge, skill, and experience in clinical social work and who agree to abide by the NASW Code of Ethics, Standards for the Practice of Clinical Social Work, and the NASW's continuing education standards. To be awarded this credential you must (1) have a CSWE-accredited MSW degree or a doctorate in social work; (2) have two years (3,000 hours) of post-MSW clinical experience in an agency or organized setting, supervised by a clinical social worker; and (3) hold a current state license or certification based on an examination (e.g., the ASWB test) or be a member of the ACSW.

The authors are disturbed that the QCSW credential formerly did not require a person to have a CSWE-accredited MSW. An individual could have earned a doctorate in social work (these are not accredited by the CSWE) without having earned an MSW (a number of doctoral programs admit students without the MSW and do not require them to earn it on the way to the doctorate). Given that the MSW is the profession's practice degree, and most doctoral programs are heavily research-oriented, this was a puzzling gap in the NASW's clinical credential. This discrepancy was brought to the attention of the NASW, and the standard was amended to read that a CSWE-accredited MSW is required.

Again, if a job requires it or provides additional benefits if you hold the QCSW credential, then by all means obtain it. However, if your state does possess strict licensure of social work practice (e.g., the

LCSW), then we think the QCSW is redundant. It may be more useful in those states with relatively weak legal regulation.

The Diplomate in Clinical Social Work

The DCSW distinguishes advanced clinical practice expertise and is NASW's highest professional clinical certification, exceeding all state requirements. The eligibility criteria are as follows:

1. Have earned a CSWE-accredited MSW degree, or a doctoral degree in social work (these are not accredited by the CSWE).
2. Document two years (3,000 hours) of postgraduate supervised clinical experience in an agency or organized setting, supervised by an experienced clinical social worker.
3. Document at least three additional years of advanced clinical practice (in addition to those noted in number two above), with at least two years of practice occurring in the previous two years.
4. Submit a completed colleague reference form.
5. Hold the highest level of social work licensure available in one's state.
6. Have passed the advanced or clinical ASWB examination.
7. Successfully complete the NASW's Diplomate Clinical Assessment Examination.
8. Affirm adherence to the NASW's Code of Ethics, Standards for the Practice of Clinical Social Work, and Continuing Education Standards.

Holders of the NASW's QCSW or DCSW credentials are eligible for listing in the association's *NASW Register of Clinical Social Workers*, a reference work sometimes used by potential clients and third party payers for referral purposes. The term *diplomate* is widely used among the practice professions (medicine, dentistry, clinical psychology, etc.), and the holder of a diplomate in a given field is generally seen as a somewhat more qualified practitioner. A related term with much the same meaning is *board certification*. For example, should one of your loved ones experience behavioral or emotional problems, having a board certified social worker would assure that the practitioner has a high level of knowledge and capability. These two terms are conflated in the following credential.

The Board Certified Diplomate in Clinical Social Work (BCD)

This credential is issued by an independent organization called the American Board of Examiners in Clinical Social Work (ABECSW), an independent group that is closely linked with the Clinical Social Work Federation, a group that is often seen as competing with the NASW for the allegiance of clinical social workers. More than thirteen thousand clinical social workers nationwide hold the BCD credential and are listed in the ABECSW's registry of clinical social workers (a different source than the NASW's similar registry), another source used by consumers and third-party payers for referral purposes. The ABECSW has its own code of ethics and advocates for increased recognition of clinical social work as a mental health specialty. To be awarded the BCD you must (1) have five years and 7,500 hours of direct clinical practice (3,000 hours under supervision); (2) have a CSWE-accredited MSW; (3) possess the highest level of social work licensure available in your state; and (4) complete the no-test application process and submit the required fee.

You can learn more about the ABECSW board-certified diplomate credential at their Web site, www.abecsw.org.

If it is confusing to you to have two diplomate programs (i.e., the DCSW and BCD) in clinical social work, it is no wonder. Back in the 1980s the ABECSW began their diplomate program, and it proved to be a very attractive program. So the NASW began its own competing diplomate. Recognizing the silliness of two essentially similar programs, wiser heads in the NASW and ABECSW prevailed, and the two groups combined their diplomate programs. The NASW and the ABECSW existed in this uneasy alliance for a couple of years and then had a major falling out. The NASW began steps to reactivate its own diplomate in clinical social work separate from the formerly jointly administered credential. The ABECSW sued the NASW and won a court injunction against the NASW that prohibited the NASW from developing a second diplomate credential for a period of five years. This ruling left the field of clinical social work diplomate credentials open to only the ABECSW system for five years. The five years transpired, and the NASW quickly recharged its diplomate program, hence we now have two very similar credentials. This is confusing to potential clients, to MSW students, and even to established members of the profession. We hope with the passage of time that only one diplomate program will be available to advanced clinical social work practitioners. Whether it be the ABECSW credential, the NASW program, a reunited joint effort of the two associations, or an entirely new initiative remains to be seen.

Meantime, worry about getting your license. Keep in mind that all these credentials and certifications afforded by various professional groups have nothing to do with licensure to practice social work.

What about Licensure as a Marriage and Family Therapist?

Many MSW students are interested in marriage and family therapy. This interest is good, as these are major fields of practice and worth pursuing as a career. However, keep in mind that the legal definition of clinical social work includes the practice of marriage and family therapy (MFT) as well as that of couples therapy, group therapy, psychotherapy, counseling, etc. You do not need licensure as a MFT in order to practice MFT. All you need is your social work license. Therefore, why go to the added trouble and expense of becoming licensed in MFT? Well, perhaps you believe that it will provide you with added expertise, clinical skills, or referrals. This may be true, but it is not a sure thing. The 1995 *Consumer Reports* study on client outcomes and satisfaction with psychotherapy found clients to be more satisfied with psychotherapy provided by social workers than by marriage counselors:

> Psychiatrists, psychologists, and social workers received equally high marks and were praised for being supportive, insightful, and easy to confide in. That remained true even when we statistically controlled for the seriousness and type of the problem and length of treatment. Those who went to marriage counselors didn't do quite as well, and gave their counselors lower grades for competence. (Staff, 1995, p. 736)

Politically you should know that segments within the MFT field are hard at work lobbying for the practice of marriage and family therapy to be limited to licensed practitioners in that discipline and for such interventions to be removed from the definition of practice of licensed social workers. Why support a separate discipline that is in part dedicated to limiting the practice of clinical social work? It is certainly possible and is a very good thing to obtain advanced training in MFT, particularly training focused on empirically supported marital and family interventions. However, we see no need for individuals otherwise qualified to be licensed clinical social workers to become licensed MFTs either in addition to, or in lieu of, their LCSW. Stick with social work.

What about Licensure as a Mental Health Counselor?

Nope. Don't bother. Although many states license professional counselors (LPC is a frequently encountered acronym), generally the standards for training and supervision are less stringent than those for licensure as a clinical social worker. Having the LPC instead of the LCSW is not a good idea if you qualify for the latter, and having the LPC in addition to the LCSW adds very little to your marketability in most practice settings. Stick with social work.

What about Becoming a Certified Addictions Counselor?

There is a movement in some circles to stress having practitioners in the fields of alcohol and substance abuse obtain an additional form of credential called the Certified Addictions Counselor (CAC). In principle, the idea of having specialized training in a given area of practice is a good one, particularly in empirically based methods of assessing and helping substance abusers. In execution, the CAC credential is sometimes not a very credible option. In many jurisdictions the academic training for the CAC is a bachelor degree or less. Some places even allow folks with a high school diploma to become a CAC. CAC embraces a disease model and the 12-step program ideology, even though this approach, while widely adopted, is not well supported in terms of validity of conceptual model or effectiveness of intervention. Many practitioners active in the substance abuse counseling field do not see addiction as a disease, per se, and do not subscribe to 12-step models of assistance. Plus, because alcoholism and substance abuse counseling is usually already incorporated into the practice prerogatives of licensed social workers, supporting the CAC credential in a way undermines the presumptive expertise of LCSWs, clinical psychologists, and psychiatrists in this area. Stick with social work. The exception of course is if your state requires some sort of separate substance abuse counselor certification, in which case you should qualify for that credential if you wish to work with this clientele.

OTHER CREDENTIALS AND CERTIFICATES

You will encounter many other tempting credentialing programs and certificates in a wide array of fields—play therapy, cognitive therapy, psychoanalysis, eye-movement desensitization and reprocessing (EMDR), neuro-linguistic programming (NLP), hypnosis, biofeedback, divorce mediation, trauma counseling, rational-emotive behavior therapy, facilitated communication, rebirthing, polarity therapy, crisis intervention, etc. Which of these options should you pursue? We suggest that you call the person who markets these programs and ask them the following simple question: "Before enrolling in your training program I would really like to learn more about (name your intervention here). Can you provide me with some current references in professional journals to credible research studies that demonstrate (name your intervention here) is effective at helping people?"

Credible programs will reply something like: "Certainly, may I have your address to mail you reprints of some articles along the lines of what you are asking about?"

Programs that are not credible will respond along the following lines: "Well, no. The powerful effects of (name the intervention here) are really too subtle to be scientifically tested"; or "Well, we have been providing this training for over X years, and have trained X thousand mental health professionals"; or "Well, all of our clients have told us that (name the intervention here) has really helped them"; or "Well, we have conducted such studies, but they are unpublished reports."

If you get the first answer, then read and critically evaluate these studies yourself. If the evidence seems adequate, then consider enrolling in the program. Consult a former faculty member if you need any assistance in judging the rigor and sophistication of a given study. If you get any answer besides the first, *do not* enroll in that program. There is no reason to waste time on the ineffective, the unproven, or the bogus.

Perhaps you think we have been too harsh in our appraisal of the value of various certifications and credentials. Maybe we have been. However, as the authors of this book we believe it is our responsibility to provide you with our honest judgements when we discuss these various alternatives. We have seen too many of our colleagues spend large amounts of time and money on useless training and credentials. One example is, (we are not making this up) learning the precise details of how to wave your fingers in the certain prescribed manner in front of an anxious client's eyes (as in EMDR), when research has shown this process to be a completely ineffectual one. The theory behind neurolinguistic programming (NLP) has been known for decades to be false, and that NLP interventions do not help clients has been clearly demonstrated in controlled studies. We have been embarrassed to find situations of LCSWs advertising the practice of polarity therapy (moving one's hands over a client's body without touching them, aligning invisible energies unknown to science); of state-board approved social work continuing education in "past-life regression therapy"; of LCSWs offering certification programs in "holotropic breathwork"; and similarly bogus interventions. We do not believe that it is too harsh to suggest that you apply the "test question" described above when considering these questionable certifications and credentials.

References

Barker, R. (Ed.). (2003). *The social work dictionary* (5th ed.). Washington, DC: NASW Press.

Ginsberg, L. H. (1998). *Careers in social work*. Boston: Allyn & Bacon.

Staff. (1995). Mental health: Does therapy help? *Consumer Reports*, November, pp. 734-739.

Thyer, B. A. (1994). Assessing competence for social work practice: The role of standardized tests. In R. G. Meinert, J. T. Pardeck, & W. P. Sullivan (Eds.), *Issues in social work: A critical analysis*. Westport, CT: Auburn House.

Thyer, B. A., & Biggerstaff, M. A. (1989). *Professional social work credentialing and legal regulation*. Springfield, IL: Charles C. Thomas.

Chapter 8

FINDING A JOB
AFTER GRADUATION

EMPLOYMENT OPPORTUNITIES IN SOCIAL WORK

Few occupations can match the sheer variety, opportunities, and settings found in social work. Social workers are found in public agencies, hospitals, courts, private practices, nursing homes, schools, clinics, police departments, private businesses, and countless other interesting workplaces. Social workers serve at all levels of government and in public agencies, private for-profit settings, voluntary settings, and non-profit settings. They are therapists, researchers, administrators, community organizers, political leaders, and legislators. Social workers work with various populations including the elderly; juveniles; young children and their families; the physically, emotionally, and mentally challenged; immigrant and refugee groups; and the poor, disenfranchised, and oppressed. Fields of practice may include child welfare, aging, public welfare, employment and occupational social work, mental health, medical social work, corrections, juvenile justice, economic services, domestic violence, probation and parole, disabilities, school social work, environmental social work, and a host of other exciting practice arenas.

Job opportunities for social workers exist in every state, across the nation, and across the globe.

FINDING THE RIGHT FIT FOR YOU IN THE JOB MARKET

You should carefully plan your job search. Before you begin job hunting, you need to think about what kind of job you want. Whether in a tight job market or in a high-demand market, thinking through some specific issues and weighing the importance of relevant factors will help you in your job search. You may already have some idea of the type of work you would like to do from your field practice experience. If you are uncertain as to the population or settings you would like to practice with, you might consider doing some of the following:

SURVIVAL STRATEGIES

- Attend meetings of your local NASW chapter to meet social workers from a variety of practice settings.
- Volunteer to work in some settings that you think may interest you.
- Ask some local social workers practicing in your community if you can interview them about what they do.
- Ask if you can spend some time observing in the agency.
- Meet with your faculty advisor to discuss career options and preferences.

It is important to be aware of your own personal considerations in your job search. A thorough and systematic job search can be extremely time consuming and energy draining. Choosing a job is influenced by many factors, including personal circumstances (such as the need to support children or the need for a flexible work schedule), professional interests (such as mental health or corrections), willingness to relocate, plans for continuing education, specialty requirements (such as licensure or certification), salary, benefits, working conditions, opportunity for advancement, and long-term career goals. You do not want to spend your time on job opportunities that you know are not well suited for you. For instance, if you know that you despise cold, wintry weather, you should not apply for a position in Iowa. If you are easily bored in a small town, focus your search on job opportunities in larger cities and urban areas. If your partner or spouse will also need to find employment or is interested in furthering his or her education, you will need to select an area that can accommodate both your job and educational needs. Remaining geographically close to aging parents or children are all important factors to consider before you begin your search. If you are fluent in a second language or interested in a new cultural experience, you may want to expand your search outside of the United States. We all have special considerations; now is the time for you (and your partner or family, if appropriate) to discuss and delineate the geographic and programmatic characteristics you want and those you do not want.

SURVIVAL STRATEGIES

- Discuss special considerations (geography, family, children, recreational opportunities) with your partner or family.
- Discuss future goals (professional, personal, educational).
- Make a list of your special considerations and keep it handy.

SEARCH METHODS

Immersed in your own search process, you may not be aware of the importance of the process and outcome from the employer's perspective. Because your relationship with the agency or organization may last for many years, most employers are keenly aware of how their hiring decisions may affect their organization, both formally and informally. This is particularly true for smaller agencies and organizations. The recruitment and hiring of professional staff can be as work intensive and emotionally charged for the people within the hiring organization as it is for you. Before you ever see an advertisement for a position vacancy, administrators and staff have probably invested a great deal of time and thought into the establishment of the position and the recruitment process.

Your most important challenge in the job hunt is to pinpoint where the jobs are. This process is very important and is a challenge that you should embrace with committed devotion. No matter how well qualified or talented you are, you must uncover the job leads to pursue them. Another less talented applicant may get that prized position that you only recently learned about simply because he or she got there ahead of you. Many organizations publish firm application closing dates. Because advertising can be expensive, some organizations may place their advertisement for only a short period of time. Consequently, you must be diligent (check for employment ads at least once a week) and thorough in your search lest you risk losing out on some outstanding opportunities.

We list several methods that you can use to assist in your search for social work positions. These include networking and attending conferences, searching the professional printed publications, conducting an electronic search, and using your professional contacts as brokers. You should use all the methods available to you.

The Traditional Search

The traditional job search includes recruitment ads, direct applications, and all the other traditional avenues to employment. Most organizations begin the search by preparing and placing an advertisement in professional newspapers such as the *NASW News* or journals read by job seekers in their discipline as well as placing advertisements in the local newspaper. Another good source of job advertisements is the local chapter newsletters of the National Association of Social Workers.

Most colleges and universities have a career services office. This office helps students through individual and group assistance to assess career alternatives, find employment, and complete a successful transition from the university to the work place. The career services office can be especially helpful for in-job placement help, which includes on-campus recruitment, job referrals, and other sources of job contacts. This university service usually holds an annual career fair providing the opportunity to speak informally with representatives from different companies about entry-level jobs and hiring practices. Career service offices may also offer workshops providing information on skills and tactics for successful interviewing, resume preparation, business and dining etiquette, and other topics. Some of these university or college career services will schedule on-campus interviews for you with companies and organizations that routinely recruit at your campus. Most career services offices maintain a job bulletin board and/or Web site posting job notices from across the country.

SURVIVAL STRATEGIES

- Review the employment section of your local newspaper every Sunday.
- Review the Sunday employment sections of newspapers from geographic areas that are of interest to you. Most libraries carry newspapers from across the nation and the world.

- Review the employment section of *NASW News*. You may either receive a copy if you are a member of NASW or you may be able to locate a copy at your library.
- Copy all advertisements that interest you. Make certain that you have all the information from the advertisement that you will need to respond to the advertisement and make application. Highlight the application deadline.
- Visit your university or college career service office. Make an appointment to see a career services advisor. Sign up for workshops on interviewing skills, resume preparation, and other pertinent workshops.
- Review the job bulletin board and/or Web site regularly.

The Electronic Search

The technological revolution is reinventing ways that people find jobs. Because of today's technology, resumes are zapped across cities or countries by telephone lines, large databases of resumes match people to jobs, help-wanted ads flash on home computer screens and CD-ROMS, and videoconferencing is used for interviewing.

The Internet, the global network of networks, has become a powerful employment medium. The Internet has empowered today's job seeker. Classified help-wanted ads and other employment information often are transmitted over online information services. Most commercial online information services have full Internet access. Your local library should have a copy of the *Gale Directory of Databases,* Vol. 1, an excellent reference listing with complete online information services available. In addition, you can find online jobs on the Internet or on electronic job bulletin boards. The ads are usually generated by companies specializing in electronic job ads, government agencies, professional societies or trade associations, and ad hoc organizations operating as a public service. Most services displaying electronic help-wanted ads deal with a wide assortment of occupations in a given field. However, you may need to be a member of a professional society or trade organization before you can use its job bulletin board.

It is expected that the Internet will be used increasingly by organizations to advertise for positions. Resource sites on the Internet provide information on all types of social work positions. The following list represents some of the most useful sites for locating social work positions.

NASW On-Line (http://naswdc.org/)

This is the online version of the *NASW News*. The social work employment line allows you to search by specialty area (aging, executive,
faculty, family/child welfare, health, mental health, and occupa-
tion/EAP) and by geographic area.

America's Job Bank (http://www.ajb.dni.us)

This site provides job listings and employer services from the Public
Employment Service, including information by state.

Job Web (http://www.jobweb.com/)

Job Web lists job resources and listings from the National Association
of Colleges and Employees.

Jobtrak (http://www.jobtrak.com/)

The Jobtrak is a job search database specifically for students and
alumni at a host of U.S. colleges and universities. Password access
is required for most listings.

Jobs in Government
(http://www.jobsingovernment.com/)

Jobs in Government allows you to search government, education, civil
service, and other public sector jobs using personal criteria. Job
descriptions, requirements, and salary are included. There is no fee
for job seekers to access Jobs in Government or to take advantage
of its resources, resume, E-mail notification, or other features.

College Grad Job Hunter (http://collegegrad.com/)

The College Grad Job Hunter is a job search guidebook to life after college for college students and recent graduates.

Chronicle Careers (http://chronicle.com/jobs/)

This is the online version of the *Chronicle on Higher Education*. This
site is for persons specifically interested in pursuing a career in
higher education. This is one of the most organized and easy to
use resources on the Internet. On average, one thousand or more
faculty positions are listed in various fields. Unfortunately, only the

current issue is available online. You should search this site weekly for appropriate position openings.

The Academic Position Network (http://www.apnjobs.com/)

The University of Minnesota Academic Position Network provides notice of national and international academic position announcements. As with *Academe This Week*, the academic institution pays a fee to post announcements on this site. However, unlike *Academe This Week*, this site continues to post an announcement until the position is filled.

The Riley Guide—Employment Opportunities and Job Resources on the Internet (http://www.rileyguide.com/)

The Riley Guide is a comprehensive list of various types of job positions. The Riley Guide is often referred to as "the grandmother of resources for job seekers." However, many organizations are not yet familiar with these resources and continue to rely on other methods of job posting. As electronic posting becomes increasingly popular, this resource will become an even more useful tool.

Social Work Search (http://www.socialworksearch.com/)

The Social Work Search site also allows you to search for positions located throughout the country. You can search in various areas including disability, mental health, direct practice, and child welfare.

Excite Job Bank (http://search.excite.com/)

The Excite Job Site allows you to search for positions located throughout the country. You may search the classifieds by profession. This job site is particularly good to search for positions in human resources and health care.

CareerBuilder.com (http://www.careerbuilder.com/)

This job site provides free access to employment ads from major U.S. newspapers. You may search by industry and location.

USAJOBS (http://www.usajobs.opm.gov/)

USAJOBS is the job site for the United States Office of Personnel Management. It is the official site for jobs and employment information.

FedWorld Federal Job Announcement Search (http://www.fedworld.gov/jobs/jobsearch.html)

This job site is a searchable database of U.S. federal job announcements.

International Federation of Social Workers (http://www.ifsw.org/Jobs.htm)

This site is an international online job bank that posts current advertisements and links to access information about career opportunities around the world.

All major newspapers' employment advertisements are also accessible via the Internet. So if you live in New York City and want to obtain a social work job in Atlanta or Seattle, a little Web-surfing can bring up the latest jobs advertised in those cities' major newspapers.

SURVIVAL STRATEGIES

- Spend time learning how to use the Internet and accessing Web sites. Pay careful attention to using the major search engines such as Yahoo, Lycos, Excite, Infoseek, and Netscape to find job Web sites throughout the country and the world. You can use any of these search engines to search for positions in almost any city or state by going to the home page of the geographic area you are interested in.
- Make a list of all the Web sites that meet your interests and geographic needs.
- Visit those Web sites at least weekly and make note of all positions that particularly interest you.

The Military

Interestingly, the military forces, specifically the U.S. Army, U.S. Navy, and U.S. Airforce all employ hundreds of MSWs. Military social workers provide mental health counseling; run community agencies on military bases; provide family support services to the families of service personnel called to serve overseas during a crisis; or for lengthy periods of time aboard ship, work as hospital social workers. Qualified MSWs can be commissioned as an officer and obtain comparatively high salaries with excellent benefits, including thirty days of annual leave per year, free continuing education programs, health care, and more. Some MSW social workers in the military get paid by the government to complete their PhDs, so consider looking into that as well.

If the rigors of military life do not appeal to you, the Department of Defense employs hundreds of civilian social workers who work on military bases alongside their military officer counterparts, again serving in a variety of roles, with comparable pay and benefits.

The United States Public Health Service is a superb career track. Can you remember Dr. Everett Koop or Dr. Jocylen Elders (former surgeon generals of the United States) giving press conferences in a naval-style uniform? That is actually the uniform of a member of the USPHS, a nonmilitary, public service career ladder dedicated to public health matters. USPHS social workers are employed at the Centers for Disease Control in Atlanta, at major hospitals around the country, and on Native American Indian reservations, etc. A little clicking and surfing on the Web will link you to these folks.

Another option is the Central Intelligence Agency. Don't scoff! You can find an advertisement from the CIA in the July 1999 issue of *NASW News*. However disconcerting it may be, apparently the CIA needs social workers to provide substance abuse counseling services for its employee assistance program. Learn about these intriguing job prospects at www.cia.gov.

Networking

Networking, the cultivation of large numbers of one-to-one contacts, is also an extremely valuable method to assist you in your job search. Word-of-mouth brokering and networking with the right people can be a powerful tool in locating positions and opening closed doors. Over time, you will develop your own network of contacts and will ask them to serve as brokers in networking on your behalf. When you are ready to enter the job market, you should write or call your professional and academic contacts, let them know of your intent to look for a position, and ask them for their help in identifying potential positions.

If you are a recent graduate or are close to finishing your graduate program, your network of useful contacts may seem small. To extend your network, begin attending professional meetings and conferences well before you are ready to enter the job market. Professional meetings and conferences such as NASW, the Association of School Social Workers, and the Mental Health Association are good places to meet and get to know your professional colleagues.

Do not overlook the potential of using the network from your own graduate program. You should tell field instructors and faculty about positions that interest you. The dean and department chair can also assist you in your search process. Ask them directly for advice and to advocate for you when appropriate. If you are interested in a specific organization or agency, find someone on your faculty who has an association with that organization and ask them to help you make contacts.

Most social work schools and departments maintain, formally or informally, a bulletin board or three-ring binder that contains job announcements, which are routinely sent by employers looking to hire MSWs. Be sure to check this resource regularly. If a regularly updated social work job bulletin board or similar arrangement containing current job listings is not maintained by your graduate program, contact your school's student-faculty affairs committee and urge them to establish such a service for its soon-to-graduate MSWs. Also, if you are moving to a new area, visit the local school of social work to see if you can use their local listings of MSW positions.

Alumni who have graduated from your program before you who are working in organizations and agencies that interest you may be helpful in your job hunt. Prior graduates tend to remain loyal to their alma maters and are often willing to assist others in being considered for a particular position.

SURVIVAL STRATEGIES

- Attend meetings of your local chapter of NASW, state clinical social work society, and other appropriate professional organizations to meet colleagues and cultivate a network.

- Attend professional conferences whenever possible. Introduce yourself to other professionals in your area of interest. Continue to meet with or correspond with them if possible.
- Meet with your faculty advisor and other faculty you know well. Tell them about your job search and ask them to help you make contacts and serve as a reference for you.
- Contact your past field instructors. Let them know of your job search and enlist them in helping you network or find position vacancies.
- Contact the dean or department chair in your department. Tell the dean or chair about your job search plans; ask them if they know of any openings and to keep you in mind.

THE JOB APPLICATION

Once you have identified some openings that interest you, you will need to be prepared to respond to the position announcements. Application materials vary across organizations, agencies, and fields of practice. Although you will usually be asked to send a cover letter, resume, and letters of recommendation, you should read each advertisement carefully for instructions, because these may vary slightly. One advertisement may request the names and addresses of three references, whereas another may require actual letters of recommendation from three references. You certainly want to communicate that you are capable of reading, understanding, and following directions. If your application is incomplete or inaccurate, it will probably be tossed aside with only a cursory review due to its failure to meet the minimal requests for the application package.

Some advertisements are not specific and may ask for a dossier or ask you to send your credentials. These general terms do not provide enough specific information for you to respond. In this case, either call the organization for more specific information or clearly note in your cover letter that you wish to be informed if they require any additional information other than what you provided.

You may also be asked to supply a transcript, examples of your writing, or copies of evaluations of your field placements. Get your application materials in order as soon as possible and add to your materials as your experience increases. Needless to say, all materials should be professionally finished and perfectly prepared. Typos, bad copies, inaccurate letters, and sloppy materials will land you in the organization's "not interested at all" category. Certainly, all work is expected to be word processed and sharply presented. A typed or handwritten resume will indicate that the applicant needs to enter the computer age. Remember, written or electronic application materials are often the only initial source of information for the search committee to consider in the selection process. This first impression is extremely important in your winning an opportunity to move to the next step in the application process.

SURVIVAL STRATEGIES

- Make a notebook containing copies of all advertised positions for which you wish to apply. Refer to this notebook frequently in preparing your applications for these positions.
- Begin to develop your resume early. Attend some resume preparation workshops at your college or university. Consult your faculty or an experienced professional colleague for guidance in preparing your resume.
- Develop a notebook of examples of your work, copies of your field evaluations, and other materials such as noteworthy certificates of accomplishment.
- Ask other professionals if you can review their resume. Select some of the best examples to use as a guide in designing your own resume.

The Cover Letter

Be prepared to send an individualized, unique cover letter to each agency or organization to which you are making an application. Many applicants use a basic word processed format and then tailor the content to the specific organization. This is a good idea; however, you need to be attentive to making appropriate changes for the new application. We have seen application packets with cover letters addressed to the correct organization but addressed to the director of a completely different organization. In another instance, an applicant addressed the cover letter to the correct person and organization, but within the body of the letter wrote excitedly of how she would like to join the group of practitioners at a competing agency. Mistakes such as these can be fatal to your job hunt, but you can avoid them by carefully proofreading your letters.

It is crucial to clearly identify your address and phone number on the cover letter. Obviously, if the search committee cannot reach you, it cannot interview you, and many reviewers will not take time to dig for your contact information. A search committee may be reviewing 100 or more applications, and so members generally do not have time to probe through materials. You may also wish to include a fax number and E-mail address if available. If you are in the process of moving, be certain to make note of this, specifying the dates and new location where you can be reached. Whatever information you decide to include, provide it in such a way that the employing organization will be able to contact you relatively easily.

If you have an answering machine that may be called by the employing organization, make sure that your message is fairly short and professional. Music, voices of your children, or other personal content is not appropriate and may be offputting to the search committee member attempting to contact you.

Your cover letter should be fairly short (generally no more than two pages) and provide sufficient information for the reviewer to become interested enough to take the time to read your resume and letters of recommendation. You must somehow convince the reviewer in this relatively short space that your application is worth continued study. Use simple, direct language, indicating some of your knowledge of the organization and how you see your expertise and qualification fitting with the organization or agency as well as with the position advertised. You should specifically note the advertised position for which you are applying, highlighting your qualifications that correspond to the position. Document your expertise in the area, and demonstrate your experience by giving examples of some of the related work you have done. This may include volunteer work, field practice experience, as well as paid employment. A cover letter can also be a good place to drop a name, if you can do it tactfully. Mentioning a faculty mentor or field instruction supervisor of local or national repute who is willing to validate your abilities can provide an important competitive edge.

SURVIVAL STRATEGIES

- Attend workshops at your college or university to learn more about writing cover letters.
- Ask close professional colleagues or faculty to share some examples of cover letters they have written.
- Write a mock cover letter and ask a trusted mentor or faculty member to critique it for you.

Preparing Your Resume

The resume (also called a *vitae*) is a factual outline of your educational and professional life. As a beginning professional, you may feel that your resume is too brief or not very impressive. Rest assured that your resume will change in the future as your productive professional life progresses. For now, you must design your resume so that it is clear and neat and so that your strongest qualifications stand out. Organize your materials carefully so that reviewers can be clear about your credentials, experience, dates of degrees received, dates of previous employment, and titles of previous positions held.

Because the appearance of your application materials is extremely important, you need to assure yourself that your resume is both clear and neat. Otherwise, it will likely be tossed aside. To help yourself in this, you might want to consider using software to produce your resume. This will give you greater flexibility in tailoring your document and will allow you to produce a quality resume at a fairly low cost. Although you do not have to have a computer program to produce a quality resume, you may want to visit a computer software store and explore what some of the computer-friendly resume writing software packages have to offer and if they would be useful to you.

Regardless of whether you use a specially designed software package or not, your resume should be word processed. Use a laser printer for the original copy of your resume. It is far better to produce multiple copies on bond paper than to rely on photocopiers.

The acceptable length of a resume varies depending on your employment history and length of time in the profession. A good resume is one that can easily be skimmed within a few seconds and yet has enough supporting detail to stand up under a careful and thorough review. Do not assume that a proper resume has to fit on only one page. A proper resume is one that concisely depicts all your relevant background and experience. Obviously a forty-five-year-old MSW student who returned to graduate school after twenty-five years in the workforce would have a more substantial resume than your typical twenty-four-year-old MSW graduate. You should organize the first page of your resume so that it contains the information about your greatest assets for the position. A resume that is not easy to skim or spot read may get short shrift among a stack of applications. Use highlighting and spacing to allow your resume to be easily sight read so that important words that best convey your qualifications and credentials jump off the page. Do not use pastel-colored or parchment-looking paper, calligraphy, an array of bizarre fonts, borders around your resume, paper with ragged edges, etc. Good quality white paper is fine. Do not encase your resume in a clear plastic binder or other cover.

All the information on your resume should be relatively straightforward. Reviewers should not have to struggle to understand it, and generally they will not take the time to attempt to calculate or guess at information. Do not in any way misrepresent yourself or your credentials on your resume. If a block of time is missing from your professional experience, it is best to address the issue in your cover letter rather than omit dates or other data from your resume. Experienced reviewers can easily detect resumes designed to obfuscate or hedge on information.

Breaking Down the Resume

Your resume should contain the following content areas: your name, current address, telephone number, fax number (if available), and E-mail address (if available). It should also contain your permanent address and phone number if you expect to be moving, information about your education, professional work experience, field placement experience, volunteer experience, research experience, community activities, professional memberships, knowledge of foreign languages; and any special honors or awards you have received. These categories usually appear in the same order on your resume as presented here. Within each of these categories, the information should be presented in reverse chronological order, from most recent backward.

Your name, address, and phone number should appear prominently at the top of the first page. Your name should also appear at the top of every page thereafter. Include both your home and office numbers if available, as well as any fax numbers or E-mail addresses that you frequently use. If you do not have an answering machine, it is a good idea to invest in one for the duration of the search process. Relying on others to convey messages is not a good idea. An answering machine allows you to retrieve your messages fairly reliably, plus it allows you to access messages pertinent to your search while you are out of town.

Education. Within this section, you should list educational work in detail from most recent backward. This should include the institution, degree, specialization or field of concentration, and date degree was received.

You may include the title of your graduation project or MSW thesis, if appropriate (if you did not complete a formal MSW thesis, do not worry). Nowadays, most MSW students do not do a formal thesis. You may also list areas of specialization, additional areas of concentration, or your involvement in other research projects.

Experience. You should include all relevant experience in this section. For each position you have held, you should include the name of the institution at which you were employed, your position title, your responsibilities and accomplishments, and the dates of employment. Depending on the extent of your experience, you may wish to include separate subsections, such as "Professional Employment Experience," "Research Experience," "Internship Experience," and "Volunteer Experience. " Provide a brief description of each item detailing the most interesting or impressive aspects of your position. Use active verb phrases, stressing your accomplishments and contributions.

Scholarly or professional memberships and leadership. In this section, you should list your memberships in scholarly or professional organizations. Many professions, particularly social work, feel very strongly about membership in the national organization of the profession. Membership in professional organizations shows your commitment to your profession and your awareness of its activities. For instance, a resume that does not indicate that the applicant is a member of the national professional organization for your field may not be considered as seriously as those of others that do list membership, especially if the applicant's qualifications are equal to or less than the others. If you are still a student, you may wish to join those professional organizations now because most provide a reduced membership rate for students.

If you have been particularly active in some organizations or in student organizations, you may also include it. It would look something like this:

> Member, National Association of Social Workers
> Graduate Student Representative, State Chapter, National Association of Social Workers
> Member, National Association of Black Social Workers
> President, Phi Alpha Honor Society

Additional Information. This is an optional section that may be used to list any special competencies or miscellaneous information you think may be important. For instance, speaking a foreign language, competency with special equipment, or knowledge in a special field should be noted in this section. Usually, information about personal factors such as hobbies, religious affiliation, marital status, and children is omitted on resumes. However, if you are disabled or a military veteran, it is appropriate to note such factors according to personal preference.

References. You may include a list of people who have agreed to write letters of recommendation or act as a reference for you. If you have a range of expertise or experience relevant to the position for which you are applying, try to include a broad range of references who can address various aspects of your experience. Although this category is optional, if any of your references are of national prominence, it can be helpful to have their names listed on your resume. Identify each reference's institution and provide phone numbers. You should select persons who know you well and know your work. Always make certain in advance that these people are willing to serve as a reference for you and will provide a positive recommendation for you.

If the advertisement requests that applicants provide letters of recommendation, then it will be your responsibility to contact your references and make certain that your recommendation letters have been sent and have arrived at the institution. First, call your references to ask them to submit letters of recommendation for you. Follow up with a written reminder reiterating the position, institution, and address. Then follow up again to be sure the letters have been received at the organization, agency, or department to which you are applying. Good references tend to be busy people—provide them with sufficient information and gentle prompting.

THE SCREENING PROCESS

The Paper Screening

Once you have applied for the positions in which you have interest and have sent each institution your cover letter, resume, and references, the institutions will conduct "paper" screenings, in which the search committees review your application materials. From the search committee's perspective, ideal candidates are those whose credentials and record of accomplishments most closely match those that the institution is seeking. Depending on the size of the applicant pool (and mission of the organization or agency) certain credentials, such as degree in hand, volunteer experience, internship experience, and specialized skills, can serve as immediate screen-in or screen-out criteria. At a minimum, you must meet the qualifications stated in the job announcement.

Next, you will be placed into one of three categories on the basis of the paper screening: in (worth pursuing), out (not worth our time), and maybe (if the in-candidates fall through, and those about whom search committee members have additional questions).

Other than meeting the minimum qualifications for the position, what kinds of considerations or judgments are made by the search committee to categorize you and the other applicants? The ideal candidate is one who represents a perfect fit between what the agency or organization needs and what the candidate offers. Obviously, each individual search committee member will make some independent judgments about your degree of fit and will assess factors such as where you did your graduate work, range of practice skills, previous experience in the field (either paid or voluntary), and specialized skills. The committee will also judge the overall visual and substantive presentation of your applications materials. Often, individual judgments made by search committee members will be discussed and rehashed with the committee, and collective decisions will be made about the relative attractiveness of the different candidates.

SURVIVAL STRATEGIES

- Ask several colleagues or your faculty advisor to provide you with some good examples of resumes. This will give you some basis on which to build your own.
- Ask several trusted colleagues or your faculty advisor to review your resume for you and give you feedback on both its content and its presentation style.
- Proofread your resume over and over again, and then once more. Any typographical or spelling errors can cause you to be dropped from consideration for the position.
- Make certain that you have included all pertinent information including any special areas of expertise, skills, awards, and honors.

A completed application is an implicit statement that you are ready to interview on short notice. Before you are even contacted, a fairly rigorous screening process has probably already taken place. If the employing institution contacts you and expresses interest, you can expect that your application has been reviewed favorably. Some agencies and organizations prioritize candidates into a short list of three to five of the top candidates and a longer list of acceptable but not top candidates. Applicants on the short list are generally contacted first.

It is not uncommon for the employing organization to contact your references and their own informal contacts who may know you to assess others' opinions of you before contacting you. Make sure your references know where you have placed your applications and for what types of positions so that they will be prepared if they are called. As mentioned previously, obtain prior approval to list someone as a reference. Never take chances; be certain that your references are prepared and willing to give you a positive recommendation. A mediocre or wishy-washy letter can at best raise a red flag and at worst be the kiss of death for your job search.

The Telephone Screen

After completing the paper screening and contacting your references, the employing organization may conduct a telephone interview with you. The telephone interview allows the organization to conduct a brief interview at low cost. The purpose is to eliminate any candidates on the short list who are no longer interested in the position, are unable to respond well to questioning, or appear inappropriate for the position despite an attractive resume. Some organizations do not use this first telephone contact as an interview but instead set up a brief face-to-face interview. In either case, this will be your first personal contact with the screening committee other than through your application materials, and at no other time during the hiring process are first impressions more important than during this brief interview.

At this point in the search process, the screening committee is assessing the extent of your interest in the position, your ability to substantiate your skills and expertise verbally as outlined on your resume, and, to some extent, your social and communication skills. The telephone screening can be a particular challenge for some applicants. Here you cannot rely on facial expressions, eye contact, or personal appearance to help you communicate. Highly qualified candidates have been known to fall flat and get eliminated because of nervousness or some other innocent interview faux pas.

When an interested organization calls, you should convey obvious pleasure at hearing from them and maintain a level of interest and enthusiasm throughout the conversation. Because this interview is so important, you might want to practice your phone interviewing skills with a colleague, friend, or mentor. Even if questions are posed differently by the interviewer, you will find that practice will aid you in providing smooth, well-thought-out responses.

SURVIVAL STRATEGIES

- Ask a faculty member, mentor, or friend to help construct questions that you can expect to be asked during the initial phone screen. Be prepared to discuss your past and current experience, future interests, as well as substantive issues in practice. Be prepared to respond to more general questions, such as your interest in the employment organization. Think through your responses to these hypothetical inquiries carefully and ask for feedback on your responses.
- Practice your responses until you feel confidence in their content as well as your phone interview style.
- Tape record and critique your responses and interview style.
- If you have applied for several positions, keep a reference log by your phone listing the individual organizations and the specific positions for which you have applied. This ready reference should also contain names of key people in the organization and any special information about the organization. Be prepared to show that you have done your homework and are somewhat knowledgeable about the organization.

The Face-to-Face Interview

Face-to-face interviews usually take place at the employing organization, either in a conference room or an office. One or more members of the search committee and an administrator may be present for the interview. In a relatively brief time frame, say one to two hours, the interviewers will attempt to assess the degree of fit between you and the organization, your ability to substantiate the skills and expertise outlined on your resume as they relate to the job position, your level of social skills, and your physical presentation style.

Some interviews may be conducted by only one interviewer, whereas others may have a fairly large group of interviewers present for the interview. It is not uncommon for several interviews to be scheduled back-to-back on the same day, with some time in between each interview for a critique of the candidate before moving on to the next applicant. Do not be surprised to find another candidate being interviewed while you are waiting for your appointment. If you are scheduled later in the day, you may find that the interviews are running late. This is not unusual and should not alarm you. Just make sure that you are on time for your appointment. If the interview is scheduled for a location you are not familiar with, scout it out ahead of time to ensure your timely arrival.

We cannot stress enough the importance of your appearance, demeanor, and interview style. Some interviewers will begin to size you up quickly based on their first impression. These first impressions are often difficult to change. Dress professionally. Men should wear a suit or, at the very least, a coat and tie. Female applicants should wear a fairly conservative suit or appropriate dress. Many applicants can share horror stories of last-minute spills or tears in stockings. Dress for the interview early enough to repair any possible problems.

Do not drink alcohol or smoke cigarettes during the interview, even if they are offered to you. Should the interview take place during a meal, order a moderately priced menu item that can be consumed with relatively little difficulty while interacting (stay away from spaghetti, thick submarine sandwiches, and other foods that tend to splash, drop, or require extensive chewing). Now is the time to remember all that your parents taught you—your dining manners and etiquette will be judged as surely as your qualifications and credentials.

To substantiate the skills and expertise outlined in your resume, you may have to answer tough, challenging questions put forth by the interviewers in a face-to-face interview. If you present yourself as an expert on a certain topic or area, the interviewers will want (and will try quickly) to establish that you are in fact an expert in that area. As with the telephone screening interviews, you should compile a list of potential questions, practice your responses, and ask a trusted colleague or mentor to critique your responses and provide you with feedback. Videotaping one or more role-played interviews can allow you to critique your nonverbal as well as verbal communication.

In addition to practicing in front of a video camera, you can improve your interviewing skills by using a computer to coach you with verbal responses. There are computerized self-tutors that can help you become skilled at job interviewing. The modestly priced software uses artificial intelligence to challenge your answers. Based on the knowledge of interviewing experts, the software is programmed to continue questioning the applicant prompted by individual responses in different creative ways. The software will critique your responses. For instance, it may suggest that you return to a certain question and improve the substance of your answer. Suppose you said that you desire a position at mental health center X because the center is geographically convenient. The software would suggest that you add to your answer. You might then respond with a statement about the outstanding reputation of the mental health center or your interest and experience in working with the types of clients they serve. The computer continues to critique your responses and provide prompts until you have given an acceptable answer to the question. Subsequent sessions pose alternative questions.

In addition to questions about education, experience, and expertise, you might be asked about your career goals, your plans over the next five to ten years, your treatment philosophy, or your approach to interdisciplinary teamwork. If you are a new graduate, with little professional work experience, you should be prepared to discuss how your graduate education prepared you for the job position.

State and federal laws protecting your privacy and individual rights forbid employers from asking questions that can lead to discrimination on the basis of race, sex, religion, national origin, or physical disability. Just because some questions are illegal does not mean that they are no longer asked. Questions regarding your marital status, plans for having children, or provisions for child care are often asked. Questions about your spouse's employment status or about your age are also illegal. Certainly there are times when such questions are asked innocently, either out of interest or in an attempt to assist you in finding a position for your spouse, finding good child care, or to introduce you to others with similar interests. You must use your best judgment in responding to these types of questions. Highlight your strengths without necessarily answering the question. If you feel uncomfortable with something being asked, you may ask the interviewer to clarify for you how the question relates to the position you are seeking.

Despite the focus of the interview, it is important that you remember that the interviewers are looking for candidates who can relate easily to other colleagues, are self-confident without being arrogant, are comfortable and pleasant in interpersonal situations, are not overly nervous or caustic, and might be someone with whom the organizational members want to have an occasional lunch. Particularly in small organizations, employees can spend a great deal of time with each other working in task groups, on committees, and in staff meetings. Collegiality and an ability to work and play well with others are important characteristics to have and to convey. Once your objective credentials and qualifications are shown to be adequate, your level of social skills and your potential for collegiality become increasingly important. It is rare for a candidate's brilliance or expertise to override demanding and generally unpleasant behavior. Many interviewers will view your ability to respond to tough questions and carry on an interesting discussion and conversation as indications of how well you will relate to others in the organization. During the interview, evidence of good social skills, including a sense of humor, can serve you well.

Related to social skills is what we call physical presentation style, a combination of physical appearance and personal mannerisms. Organization and agency environments are microcosms of the larger societal environment, and personal biases, prejudices, and mannerisms are rampant. If we think of appearance and mannerisms as existing on a continuum, then extremes on either end are probably the most problematic for many organizations. For example, if you are extremely well dressed, you may fit in as poorly as you would if you were extremely poorly dressed. Likewise, being extremely young or extremely old, extremely conservative in appearance or extremely liberal in appearance, and extremely overweight or extremely underweight all potentially make you a less attractive candidate. Extreme or unusual mannerisms, such as a very loud or unusual laugh, very rapid or slow speech, and obvious nervous gestures, are also potential strikes against you.

What difference to an individual's ability to practice would any of these physical attributes make? Of course, mostly none is the answer. The reason they become problematic is that they draw attention to you and often result in people around you becoming uncomfortable. If you are clearly the most outstanding candidate in the applicant pool, then some of these characteristics might be overlooked. On the other hand, if the pool is otherwise strong or there is at least one other equally qualified candidate, these kinds of attributes can eliminate you from consideration.

Often the last ten to fifteen minutes of the interview are left to provide the applicant with an opportunity to ask questions. Many applicants are not prepared for this opportunity and are often left uncomfortably searching for something to say. This is a good time to demonstrate your familiarity with the organization or agency. This can be done very appropriately in the context of your acknowledgment of a desire to establish the degree of fit between you and the employing organization. Be prepared with some questions that communicate your desire to learn more about the organization, while determining how you could best fit in. At this point, you should probably stay away from any specific hiring questions such as salary and work load. However, you may ask for a sense of the timing of the search and when the committee will be moving to the next step in the process. Take advantage of the individual interview to communicate your interest in the position and the organization. Make certain to point out at least one positive view you have gained since speaking with the interviewing committee. At the end of the interview, be sure to shake hands with each member of the interview party, smile, and look at them while expressing your appreciation for the interview. The day after the interview, you should send a brief note to each member of the interviewing party to thank them and reiterate your continued interest in the position.

SURVIVAL STRATEGIES

- Develop a list of questions that might be asked in the face-to-face job interview.
- Practice answering these questions and ask a friend or mentor to role-play the job interview with you.
- After you feel confident, videotape the role-play. Ask a friend or mentor to help critique your role-play. Pay special attention to your nonverbal communication as well as the content of your answers.

- Select your clothing for the interview ahead of time. Make sure your clothing is cleaned and pressed. You may want to ask a trusted friend or mentor for advice regarding your selection of clothing for the interview.
- Scout out the interview site ahead of time so that you will be certain that you know how to get there and how much travel time to allow yourself so that you will arrive for the interview on time.
- Make a list of potential questions you might ask at the close of the interview.
- Practice, practice, practice your interviewing.

NEGOTIATING A JOB OFFER

After all your hard work in the search and interviewing process, you now find yourself sitting by the phone waiting for an offer. This can be a particularly difficult time, but don't just sit there! Continue your search; new positions are advertised continuously. Continue to apply for those that interest you. Contact all your references, colleagues, and advisors. Let them know of your interviews and recent applications. Continue to express interest by writing letters to those organizations you are interested in. However, do not write or call so frequently that you become a nuisance or, worse, that you appear desperate.

If you have been diligent in your search and carefully prepared for your interviews, you will no doubt receive a phone call offering you a job. Most offers are first made by telephone. The initial phone call is usually for the purpose of sounding out the likelihood of acceptance and to begin discussing some practical details. Always express pleasure at hearing from the organization or agency, and avoid making a commitment right away. You will want time to consider the offer. Most likely, the organization will give you time to consider the offer and make a decision. Any time between a few days to two weeks is fairly common. You should feel comfortable asking the organization how long it plans to give you to make your decision. Be sure to convey enthusiasm at the same time that you are requesting some time to consider the offer. Remember, no offer is final until you receive it in writing. Although instances of withdrawn verbal offers are rare, there have been instances where job candidates have become so aggressive, demanding, or unreasonable during the negotiations that the employing organization has withdrawn its offer.

The first call you receive may be a preliminary call to assess your continued interest in the position, to reassure you of their continued interest in you, or to begin initial discussions regarding the job offer. The second call is generally more definite and specific in nature, with at least a statement that you will be made an offer for the position. You should be prepared to ask questions when you receive the offer, or very soon after. We suggest that you make a list of questions as soon as you return from your initial interview. If you have interviewed with several different organizations, you may confuse issues or forget some critical questions pertaining to a specific job position. Because you will have different questions for each employing organization, you will need to make a separate list for each position and employing organization. Having a list of questions readily available when the employer calls is vitally important. It is not good to call the employer over and over again to ask questions. You will appear disorganized, nit-picky, and greedy. Busy administrators do not have time to constantly respond to your phone calls, no matter how much they may wish to hire you. Avoid asking trivial questions, and focus on issues that are serious negotiating points for you. Remember to stay enthusiastic and pleasant in your discussions. You do not want the administrator to regret the decision to offer you the position.

Some interviews are extremely informative, whereas others yield little information about the general operating procedures of the organization. If you have important questions about organizational functioning that are not necessarily related to the negotiation of the job offer, you should begin asking those questions after the organization has clearly expressed interest in extending you an offer. Make it clear that these are points of interest and understanding, and not necessarily related to negotiating the offer. For instance, you may wish to ask for copies of the personnel policies and procedures, the by-laws of the organization, and policies regarding support for continued education. There are other important details you will want to know as well. For instance, make sure you know where your office will be located. You may want to find out how much traveling will be expected of you.

The actual job offer is written by the administrator of the organization or the head of human resources. Do not consider yourself hired until the offer has been negotiated and you have received and replied to a written offer. Negotiation begins after you have received the verbal offer and ends after you have signed and returned the written offer. This is the time that you are in the strongest position to ask for salary or other special conditions that may be important to you. First, it is important that you understand all the details behind the job offer before you accept. These questions can and should be posed in a manner that appears to reflect your excitement and enthusiasm about joining the organization. These questions should not appear as quibbling. Final negotiating criteria usually include such things as salary, position title, terms of employment conditions, work load, work hours, moving expenses, and support for continued education or professional development. You must clearly decide on negotiating issues that are important to you. Discuss these issues thoroughly with pertinent others (such as a spouse or partner who may be affected by your new job), and specify the issues on a list by priority for your reference during the negotiation. This is important because negotiating an offer can be extremely stressful or uncomfortable. You do not want to forget your important negotiating issues or appear to be confused during the negotiation process. Remember to maintain a pleasant demeanor throughout the negotiation. Most important, do not rush into any agreements you will regret later.

Be prepared to assess the appropriateness of the salary initially offered to you by knowing the salary ranges for the type of position and organization. National salary studies are frequently published and available through the National Association of Social Workers. Think very carefully before deciding to accept a position. Accepting an offer can provide an immediate relief for your current unemployment status, but an ill-made match can be devastating for you and the employing institution. Verbally accepting a position and subsequently rejecting the offer can have serious long-term repercussions for your reputation.

If you have decided to accept a position offered verbally over the phone, immediately send a letter confirming your acceptance and outlining any pertinent details discussed in your phone conversation. Be sure to convey your delight at the prospect of joining the organization and that you are looking forward to receiving the written letter of offer.

Upon receipt of the written letter of offer, read the details carefully, and, if it is in agreement with your verbal discussions and negotiations, sign the letter and return it before the expiration date of the offer. Once you have signed and returned a written letter of offer, your bargaining leverage will significantly decline, and the organization will most likely consider this phase of the search process closed. You should immediately inform your references, the career placement bureau (if you used one), and other organizations considering you for a position that you are no longer on the job market.

If you find yourself in the position of rejecting an offer, you are probably doing so because you have accepted another offer, you do not find the offer acceptable, or you are not interested in joining that particular organization. Despite your reasons for rejecting an offer, always do so graciously and express appreciation for the organization's interest in you. Be careful not to burn any bridges. Thank the committee for the offer and their interest in you. If you are accepting another position, let the organization know where you will be going. Consider sending a personal note of thanks to the search committee chair.

SURVIVAL STRATEGIES

- Make a list of all questions you may have for each position for which you have applied. Keep this list by the phone.
- Review national and regional salary guidelines through the National Association of Social Workers.
- Thoroughly discuss any job offers with your partner or significant others who may be affected by your acceptance.
- Carefully review the written letter of offer before signing.
- Once you have accepted a position, contact your references to let them know that you have accepted a position. Contact all organizations to which you have applied to let them know that you are no longer available for a position.

As you can see from reading this chapter, there is a variety of exciting and rewarding job opportunities in social work. Finding a job upon graduation can be both exciting and stressful. It is very important that you put your best foot forward throughout the job hunt process. From the application to the interview to negotiating the job offer, you need to remember that every impression you make is important. We urge you to use all of the resources available to you during this process. Ask your peers and the professionals at the career center to review your application materials and resume before you send them out. Ask a few faculty and persons from the career center to conduct a mock interview with you to give you some experience and familiarity with the interview process. And, when you are negotiating that all-important job offer, give yourself time to think through all of the issues carefully before proceeding with the negotiation.

Appendix

PROFESSIONAL SOCIAL WORK ORGANIZATIONS

A significant part of your socialization into the social work profession will consist of activities you engage in *apart from* those associated with your formal MSW program, or even your post-MSW work experience. We are talking about your membership and active participation in one or more of the many professional social work organizations. Such groups can be very broad or very narrow in scope, and there is likely some association that has been established by and for social workers who share your particular professional interests. We strongly believe that active membership in such professional social work organizations, even as an MSW student, is an excellent way to become more fully integrated into the community of MSWs and others active in a given field of practice.

The bulk of this section consists of a selective listing of professional social work organizations that we think will be helpful to MSW students. Some of our descriptions of these various groups came from the *Social Work Dictionary*, edited by Robert Barker (2003), and others from various Web pages maintained by different groups. We were not successful in tracking down complete postal mailing addresses for every group, along with phone numbers and E-mail addresses. Unfortunately, these bits of information are constantly changing, which makes providing up-to-date information somewhat of a challenge. Please note that this section does not provide a comprehensive listing—there are many more groups available for you to join than we could possibly enumerate. Second, this is a disciplinary listing of organizations about social work. It is not a listing of interdisciplinary groups, organizations composed of folks who share an interest in, say, a given field of practice or method of intervention, but rather it is intended to describe social work associations.

For example, the interdisciplinary group called the Association for Behavior Analysis is not listed because this group consists of psychologists, educators, social workers, and others interested in the interventions known as behavior analysis, but it is not only a social work group. Similarly, the Child Welfare League of American, a worthy organization embraced by members of many disciplines, also did not make the cut because it focuses on a field of practice, child welfare. This is not to say that you should not seriously consider joining these interdisciplinary groups—you should join them if they are relevant to your professional interests. Some of them maintain special interest groups composed exclusively of social workers, and a few of these are quite large. For example, the American Public Health Association supports a large membership division for social workers, as does the American Association on Mental Retardation. You can attend the APHA or AAMR annual conventions and spend your time attending social work paper presentations and networking with social workers.

In the interests of fairness we list and describe these selected groups in alphabetical order, not in their order of importance. In fact, the very last group mentioned, the Society for Social Work and Research, is a particular favorite of both authors.

American Association of Spinal Cord Injury Psychologists and Social Workers

This is a professional membership organization composed of psychologists and social workers who practice in the field of spinal cord injury. They sponsor an annual conference and newsletter. They may be contacted at:

American Association of Spinal Cord Injury
Psychologists & Social Workers
75–20 Astoria Blvd.
Jackson Heights, NY 11370-1177
Voice: (718) 803-3782
Fax: (718) 803-0414

American Network of Home Health Care Social Workers, Inc.

This group is a professional association organized for the benefit of social workers employed in home health care settings. Any person, agency, or organization with an interest in home health care and a willingness to adhere to the policies and bylaws of the American Network is welcome to become a member by paying dues. You may contact this group using the following information:

American Network of Home Health Care Social Workers
1187 Wilmette Avenue, #139
Wilmette, IL 60091
Voice: (847) 853-9204
Fax: (847) 853-9276

Association for the Advancement of Social Work with Groups

The AASWG is a membership group open to social workers and others interested in group work and group therapy. It sponsors a Web-based discussion list, national newsletter, chapters in many states, an annual conference, and educational materials such as model course syllabi related to groups. It also advocates for a greater role for group work in the social work curriculum. You may contact them via:

Association for the Advancement of Social Work with Groups
c/o The University of Akron
Akron, OH 44325-8050
URL: www.aaswg.org

Association for Community Organization and Social Administration

This is a professional membership association for those concerned with social intervention at the macrolevel. Its members include community organizers, planners, administrators, policy practice specialists, and activists from a variety of disciplines and professional fields. ACOSA sponsors the *Journal of Community Practice* and the *ACOSA Newsletter*, sponsors an annual convention, and is a vital voice for social workers concerned with promoting system-wide change. You can contact ACOSA using the following information:

ACOSA Membership Department
20560 Bensley Avenue
Lynwood, Illinois 60411
Voice: (708) 757-4187
Fax: (708) 757-4234

E-mail: akj@uic.edu
URL: www.acosa.org

Association of Oncology Social Work

The AOSW is dedicated to increasing awareness about the social, emotional, educational, and spiritual needs of cancer patients. It supports its members' commitment to helping and advocating for cancer patients by providing continuing education through conferences and publications, promoting clinical research, and fostering networking to address common issues and concerns. It is involved in numerous collaborative efforts with other national and international oncology organizations to advocate for the support and care of people with cancer. It offers annual awards such as the "Oncology Social Worker of the Year" award. Contact them using the following information:

Association of Oncology Social Workers
100 North 20 Street, 4th Floor
Philadelphia, PA 19103
Voice: (215) 599-6093
Fax: (215) 545-8107
URL: www.aosw.org

Canadian Association of Social Workers

This group is the Canadian equivalent to the U.S. NASW. They are a national voice of more than thirteen thousand social workers and produce the *Canadian Social Work Journal*, a newsletter, a code of ethics, policy and position papers, reports, and books. For further information contact:

Canadian Association of Social Workers
383 Parkdale Avenue, Suite 402
Ottawa, ON K1Y 4R4 Canada
Voice: (613) 729-6668
Fax: (613) 729-9608
E-mail: casw@casw-acts.ca
URL: www.casw-acts.ca/

Clinical Social Work Federation

The Clinical Social Work Federation is a confederation of thirty-one state societies of clinical social workers. These state societies are formed as a voluntary association for the purpose of promoting the highest standards of professional education and clinical practice. Each society is active with legislative advocacy and lobbying efforts for adequate and appropriate mental health services and coverage at their state and national levels of government. Beyond supporting the state societies' aims, the board of the CSWF seeks to keep clinical social work visible and understood, to generate clinical research, and to provide professional training and publications on the national level.

The CSWF (formerly known as the National Federation of Societies for Clinical Social Work) is the largest organization of social workers solely devoted to clinical social work. It sponsors the *Clinical Social Work Journal*, a newsletter, periodic national conventions, and its state chapters usually hold conferences. The CSWF also supports an advanced practice credential (via its affiliate, the American Board of Examiners in Clinical Social Work) called the Board Certified Diplomate in Clinical Social Work, for which clinical social workers with several years of appropriately supervised practice experience may apply. No written test is required to obtain this credential. You can contact the CSWF using the following information:

Clinical Social Work Federation
P.O. Box 3740
Arlington, VA 22203
Voice: (703) 522-3866
Fax: (703) 522-9441
URL: www.cswf.org

An affiliate of the CSWF is the National Membership Committee on Psychoanalysis in Clinical Social Work, Inc., for those interested in this modality of practice. You will need to complete an application to join. At the time of publication, the current contact was:

Laurie E. Curtis, MSW
Membership Chair, NMCPSW
6420 Willow Wood Road
Edina, MN 55436
Voice: (612) 493-0171
E-mail: Lauriealan@aol.com
URL: www.nmcop.org

Computer Use in Social Services Network

These folks are the techies of social work. It is an informal association of professionals interested in exchanging information and experiences on using computers in human services. The association has been in existence since 1981 and sponsors the *Journal of Technology in Human Services* (formerly *Computers in Human Services*), periodic national and international conferences, and supports training outlines, workshops, and presentations. If you like computers and other types of advanced technology as applied to social work, this is the group for you. To subscribe to CUSSNET, the Listserv for this informal group, type **subscribe cussnet your first name your last name** in the subject line and e-mail to listserv@listserv.uta.edu. Their URL is www2.uta.edu/cussn/cussn.html

Council of Nephrology Social Workers

This group of folks consists of medical social workers who specialize in the field of nephrology (kidney diseases and kidney transplantation). The CNSW is sponsored by the National Kidney Foundation and provides all members with a subscription to the *Journal of Nephrology Social Work*, the *CNSW Quarterly Review*, and other newsletters, and also with research opportunities, annual conferences and other meetings, special mailings, and educational materials. Dues are $25 per year for student members. To join CNSW, please contact:

National Kidney Foundation
Membership Department
30 East 33rd Street
New York, NY 10016
Voice: (212) 889-2210
Fax: (800) 622-9010
E-mail: joinNKF@kidney.org
URL: www.kidney.org

Council on Social Work Education

The purpose of the CSWE is to provide national leadership and collective action designed to ensure the preparation of competent and committed social work professionals. This includes promoting and maintaining the quality of social work education programs. It also includes stimulating the development of knowledge, practice, and service effectiveness designed to promote social justice and further community and individual well-being. MSW students may join as associate members. The CSWE holds a yearly convention (during the winter), called the annual program meeting, and publishes the quarterly *Journal of Social Work Education*, a periodic newsletter, and books related to social work education. It also provides other services such as a employment registry for academic social workers, compilations of syllabi on particular topics, and related educational activities.

Council on Social Work Education
1600 Duke Street, Suite 300
Alexandria, VA 22314-3421
Voice: (703) 683-8080
Fax: (703) 683-8099
URL: www.cswe.org

International Federation of Social Workers

The IFSW is a global organization that strives for social justice, human rights, and social development through the development of social work, best practices, and international cooperation between social workers and their professional associations. Regular membership in the IFSW is available only to organizations (like the NASW, to which you already likely belong). However, they have an IFSW Friends program, which you join as an individual. The IFSW sponsors a biennial international conference, publishes a newsletter, consults with the United Nations on human rights matters, and generally serves as a networking medium for social workers with international interests.

International Federation of Social Workers
P.O. Box 4649, Sofienberg, N-0506
Oslo, Norway
URL: www.ifsw.org
E-mail: secr.gen@ifsw.org

National Association of Black Social Workers

The NABSW, established in 1968, consists of black social workers and other social workers who are interested in the goals of the organization. These goals are to deal with the problems pertinent to the black community at all levels, including working with clients, promoting programs that serve African Americans, and assisting black social workers. The NABSW holds annual conventions and publishes the journal *Black Caucus* and a newsletter. You may contact the NABSW at:

National Association of Black Social Workers
1220 11th Street NW, Ste. 2
Washington, DC 20001
URL: www.nabsw.org

National Association of Perinatal Social Workers

This organization is composed of medical social workers who have specialized in the psychosocial treatment of the mother, fetus, and newborn. Perinatal social workers are employed primarily in hospital settings and maternity medical facilities, but many also serve in public health settings, AIDS clinics, ethics centers, and private practice. You may contact the NAPSW at:

National Association of Perinatal Social Workers
c/o Irene Bruskin, NAPSW Membership Chair
3959 Broadway CHN T 757
New York, NY 10032
URL: www.napsw.org

National Association of Puerto Rican/ Hispanic Social Workers

This is a group of professional social workers of Hispanic heritage whose members work primarily toward the improvement of social conditions for Hispanics and for the professional goals of Hispanic social workers. The group was originally established in 1971 as the National Association of Puerto Rican Social Service Workers. You can contact them at:

NAPRHSW
Pauline Velazquez, membership information
P.O. Box 651
Brentwood, NY 11717
Voice: (631) 864-1537
URL: www.naprhsw.org

National Association of Social Workers

The National Association of Social Workers is the oldest and largest professional organization for social workers. Applicants should have a BSW, an MSW, or a doctorate in social work, or be a student (like you!) in a CSWE-accredited program leading to a BSW or MSW or in a doctoral social work program (these are not accredited by the CSWE). You will likely be required to join the NASW as a student member when you matriculate as an MSW student, the reason being that your program will require you to have malpractice liability insurance prior to beginning practicum, and the most available, low-cost form of such insurance is offered via membership in the NASW.

The NASW is an immense association, with many diverse activities. One good way to get oriented about it is to read the entry in the 1995 edition of the *Encyclopedia of Social Work* by Goldstein and Beebe, which describes the NASW and provides a good overview of the group's missions, history, structure, national committees, and credentialing programs. Another good source of information is the NASW Web site, www.naswdc.org, which contains more current information, such as the development of specialty sections and the addresses of the various state chapters of the NASW (which you will automatically belong to by virtue of joining the NASW). The NASW Web page also is a good place to locate Internet-based links to the Web pages of a large number of other social work-related organizations.

Consider becoming involved in the NASW through various activities, such as attending its national, regional, or state conferences; attending local chapter meetings; presenting papers at these various meetings; running for office (many positions are open to student members or representatives); submitting letters to editors of NASW journals and newsletters; or even submitting essays, editorials, or articles to these outlets. The NASW has an emerging system of sections, special interest groups, or divisions within the larger organization consisting of NASW members with similar interests. At present there are sections you may join that are devoted to the fields of aging; alcohol, tobacco, and other drugs; and school social work, among others.

The NASW has an active publishing arm, the NASW Press, which produces the journals *Social Work* (which you will receive as an automatic membership benefit), *Social Work Research, Health and Social Work, Children & Schools*, (formerly called *Social Work in Education*), and *Social Work Abstracts*; an ongoing stream of social work books related to policy, practice, research, and theory; the national newsletter *NASW News* (which you will also automatically receive); and other resources, such as the aforementioned *Encyclopedia of Social Work* and a membership directory. You will likely receive (by virtue of being a student member of the NASW) a publications catalog of the NASW Press, which will tell you about all the current NASW products and how to order or subscribe to them. You can contact the NASW at:

National Association of Social Workers
750 First Street, NE, Suite 700
Washington, DC 20002-4241
Voice: (202) 408-8600
Toll-free voice: (800) 742-4089
URL: http://www.naswdc.org

North American Association of Christians in Social Work

The NAACSW describes itself as a "vital Christian presence in social work." It sponsors a journal (*Social Work and Christianity*), a newsletter (*Catalyst*), a national conference, professional liability insurance, a continuing education program, and a job-finding service for Christian social workers. Membership requires signing a statement of faith and practice. You may contact the NAACSW at:

North American Association of Christian Social Workers
P.O. Box 121
Botsford, CT 06404-0121
Toll-free voice: (888) 426-4712
E-mail: nacsw@aol.com
URL: www.nacsw.org

National Network for Social Work Managers

The NNSWM is the only professional association in America dedicated solely to equipping social work managers to become effective "people-centered" leaders. It provides training in human services management, networking opportunities, national and regional conferences, sponsors the *Administration in Social Work* journal, and the *Social*

Work Executive quarterly newsletter, publishes a membership director, and gives out various awards. You may contact this group at:

The National Network for Social Work Managers
c/o Jane Addams College of Social Work
M/C 309, 1040 W. Harrison St.
Chicago, IL 60607
URL: www.socialworkmanager.org

National Organization of Forensic Social Work

The National Organization of Forensic Social Work (NOFSW) was established to provide for the advancement of education in the field of forensic social work through training programs, forums, panels, and lectures. It also provides an annual conference, an advanced practice credential called the Diplomate in the Academy of Forensic Social Work, a newsletter, networking opportunities, and political advocacy. Forensic social work is the application of social work to questions and issues relating to law and legal systems. Litigation (both criminal and civil), child custody issues, spouse abuse, juvenile and adult justice services, corrections, and mandated treatment all fall under the scope of this group. For more information about the National Organization of Forensic Social Work, contact:

NOFSW National Office
2600 Dixwell Avenue, Suite 7
Hamden, CT 06514
URL: www.nofsw.org

School Social Work Association of America

The SSWAA is dedicated to promoting the professional development of school social workers in order to enhance the educational experience of students and their families. Among its goals are supporting a nationwide network of school social workers, influencing public policy, and sponsoring an annual conference, a Web page, and a Listserv. The official publication of the SSWAA is the *MINI-bell* and is published quarterly. Contact this organization at:

School Social Work Association of America
P.O. Box 2072
Northlake, IL 60164
URL: www.sswaa.org

Society for Social Work and Research

The Society for Social Work and Research is among the newest, most vibrant, and exciting social work organizations you can join. It was established in 1994 as a freestanding membership association dedicated to improving the support for research among social workers. Membership benefits include a subscription to the bimonthly *Research on Social Work Practice* journal (which is edited by one of the authors of this book); reduced registration fees for the annual conference; receipt of the *SSWR Newsletter*; inclusion in the SSWR membership directory; and eligibility to participate in the SSWR mentor program. The SSWR also supports a comprehensive research awards program. Student membership dues are only $50, so joining the SSWR is a terrific deal. To join, see www.sswr.org.

So you now have a brief overview of a number of professional social work organizations you may elect to join. You will likely be impressed with the diversity of what we social workers do and by your options for professional affiliations. You are eligible to become a member of most of them by virtue of being an MSW student. Student dues are usually quite low, a teaser-rate, designed to entice you into the organization, and be so happy with your membership that you will agree to pay the much more substantial dues required of those who have graduated with their MSW degree, once you finish school.

As you begin to narrow your practice interests and outline professional goals, membership in one or more of these generalist or specialist groups may prove to be quite attractive to you. Active participation, apart from simply paying your annual dues, can be quite rewarding. Most groups rely heavily on the voluntary services of members like you to keep things happening. Before you know it you can be elected to a leadership role, if that interests you, or simply be content serving as a worker-bee, staffing a registration desk at an annual meeting, helping select papers to be read at a convention, or updating and mailing a membership registry. Someone does these things, and be assured, your offer to help will not go ignored. We, the authors, have done all these tasks in the past, and we do these things now. And we encourage you to do so as well. You will reap immense benefits from joining and being active in professional associations, such as those outlined in this chapter.

Membership in professional associations is not always a blessing. Many times the persons or policies associated with a given social work group will make you want to hold your nose in disgust. It is an individual judgement call for you to determine the extent to which the rewards outweigh the detriments of joining a given group and directly supporting all their actions via your dues payments, even those you disagree with on the basis of philosophical or ethical principles. You may encounter social workers, even among your faculty, who will disparage membership in a given professional association because of some perceived slight, mishap, or even a serious ethical problem. Sometimes rival associations compete for your interest and support by criticizing the other group. You should neither discount nor believe all such negative appraisals. The best course of action is to use your own intellect to collect the facts, weigh the evidence, and integrate this with your personal experiences. All of these groups are composed of well-educated and well-intentioned folks. They really do want to do the right thing. Occasionally, a bad apple (or episode) taints a group for a while, but you should judge this against the larger pool of good works performed by the group as a whole.

We have undoubtedly not described a large number of important social work organizations which MSW students could join. Please rest assured that any omissions are solely due to our inability to readily find sufficient information, including addresses, about them and not from a bias against certain groups on our part. If you know of additional social work membership groups that welcome MSW students, please feel free to contact us and we will be sure to include these associations in a future edition.

Congratulations on making it through this book, and presumably nearing the end of your MSW training. Although this marks the end of one aspect of your education—learning how to be a social worker—it also marks the beginning of another phase of your professional development. Now you can relax and enjoy the rigors of a new MSW-level job, obtain appropriate supervision that can be used for eventual licensure, and consider various in-service and continuing education programs. It never ends. We would like to know what you think about this book and how we can improve it during future editions. You can E-mail Bruce directly at Bthyer@fsu.edu. You have our best wishes as you embark on the adventurous career of social work.

References

Barker, R. (Ed.). (1999). *The social work dictionary* (4th ed.). Washington, DC: NASW Press.

Blount, M. (1996). Social work practice with Native Americans. In D. F. Harrison, B. A. Thyer, & J. S. Wodarski (Eds.), *Cultural diversity and social work practice* (2nd ed., pp. 257-298). Springfield, IL: Charles C. Thomas.

Goldstein, S., & Beebe, L. (1995). National Association of Social Workers. In R. Edwards (Ed.), *Encyclopedia of social work* (pp. 1747-1764). Washington, DC: NASW Press.

INDEX